SALMON

INTERNATIONAL CHEFS' RECIPES

Editor: Willy Wyssenbach

Photographs by Terje Marthinusen · Oslo

SALMON

INTERNATIONAL CHEFS' RECIPES

ST. MARTIN'S PRESS
NEW YORK

Salmon
International Chefs' Recipes

© Gyldendal Norsk Forlag A/S Oslo
1986.
Published in co-operation with
Markedsrådet for norsk laks,
Olav Tryggvasonsgt. 39/41,
N-7000 Trondheim.
English translation © 1987 by
Gyldendal Norsk Forlag A/S.

First U.S. Edition published in 1987 by
St. Martin's Press Inc.,
175 Fifth Avenue,
New York, N.Y. 10010.

Library of Congress Catalog Card
Number: 87-043073
ISBN 0-312-00715-9

First UK edition published in 1987 by
Ebury Press
Division of The National Magazine
Company Ltd.,
Colquhoun House
27-37 Broadwick Street
London W1V 1FR

ISBN 0 85223 623 9

First published in Norway by
Gyldendal Norsk Forlag A/S,
under the title
*Norwegian Salmon:
International Chefs' Recipes.*

Translation by
Jacques Delourme M.A., Jaren

Design by
Josef Leupi, Stabekk

Menu photograph credits:

China dinner plates and serving dishes:
Porsgrunds Porselænsfabrik A/S,
Porsgrunn

Crystal glasses:
Hadeland Glassverk, Jevnaker

Food preparation:
Willy Wyssenbach
and Hans Robert Bruun,
Continental, Oslo

Pages 22-23, 26-27, 48-49:
W. Yang, A/S Restaurant Tokyo, Oslo

Typesetting by A/S Idémølla, Oslo

Printed in Denmark by
Aarhuus Stiftsbogtrykkerie, Århus 1987

We will imagine that it is the middle of June, and that London has begun to be as intolerable as it usually becomes at that season, and that my reader is willing to fly with me across the sea and to settle down for a space in a Norwegian valley, and surrounded by scenery unsurpassed in its abrupt wildness by anything to be seen even in that wildest of wild countries, survey salmon-fishing from an Anglo-Norwegian sportsman's point of view. Having with more or less discomfort safely run the gauntlet of that most uncertain and restless of oceans, the North Sea, we land at the head of the Romsdal Fjord, and after about an hour's carriole drive are deposited, stunned and bewildered by the eccentricities which stupendous and impossible Nature has erected all around us, at the door of a clean, pine-built, whitepainted house, in the midst of what looks like the happy valley of Rasselas; surrounded by bright green meadows, walled in by frowning impracticable precipices 2.000 feet high at their lowest elevation, and over 4.000 at their highest, at the top of

which, opposite the windows to the southwest, even as exclusive mortals garnish their walls with broken bottles, so Nature appears to have wished to throw difficulties in the way of some gigantic trespasser by placing a fearful chevaux-de-frise of strange, sharp, jagged, uncouth and fantastic peaks, which baffle all description in their dreamy grotesqueness. These are called by the natives "Troll tinderne" i.e. "witch peaks", or "sorcerers' seats".

It is the river Rauma out of which I want my reader to catch a salmon, or see me catch one. It flows down the middle of the valley, not as Scottish rivers, London or Dublin porter-hued, but clear, bright, and translucent as crystal.

Here, amid such scenes, with this glorious stream rushing tumultuously in a sort of semicircle round me, thus giving me some half-a-dozen salmon pools, each within about 200 yards from the house, have I provided myself with a dwelling and an estate.

I have great faith in myself today, and feel that great things are still in store for me. I recommence operations, and with some success, for I land a twelve and a sixteen pounder in a very short space of time; after which, towards the tail of this great pool, I hook something very heavy and strong, which runs out my line in one rush almost to the last turn of the reel before my Norwegian friend Ole can get way on the boat to follow him, and then springs out of the water a full yard high; this feat being performed some 120

Isfjorden by Åndalsnes

yards off me, and the fish looking even at that distance enormous. I have no doubt that I have at last got fast to my ideal monster — the seventy-pounder of my dreams. Even the apathetic Ole grunts loudly his "Gud bevarr!" of astonishment.

I will spare the reader all the details of the struggle which ensues, and take him at once to the final scene, some two miles down below where I hooked him, and which has taken me about three hours to reach — a still back-water, into which I have with extraordinary luck contrived to guide him, dead-beat. No question now about his size. We see him plainly close to us, a very porpoise. I can see that Ole is demoralised and unnerved at the sight of him. He had twice told me, during our long fight with him, that the fortythree pounder of this morning was "like a small piece of this one" — the largest salmon he had ever seen in his fifty years' experience; and to my horror I see him, after utterly neglecting one or two splendid chances, making hurried and feeble pokes at him with the gaff — with the only effect of frightening him by splashing the water about his nose.

In a fever of agony I bring him once again within easy reach of the gaff, and regard him as my own. He is mine now! he *must* be! "Now's your time, Ole — can't miss him! — now — now!

He does though! and in one instant a deadly sickness comes over me as the rod springs straight again, and the fly dangles useless in the air. The hold has broken. Still the fish is so beat that he lies there yet on his side. He knows not he is free! "Quick, gaff him as he lies. Quick! do you hear? You can have him still!" Oh, for a Scotch gillie! Alas for the Norwegian immovable nature! Ole looks up at me with lack-lustre eyes, turns an enormous quid in his cheek, and does nothing. I cast down the useless rod, and dashing at him wrest the gaff from his hand, but it is too late. The huge fins begin to move gently, and he disappears slowly into the deep!

Yes — yes, he is gone! For a moment I glare at Ole with a bitter hatred. I should like to slay him where he stands, but have no weapon handy, and also doubt how far Norwegian law would justify the proceeding, great as is the provocation. But the fit passes, and a sorrow too deep for words gains possession of me, and I throw away the gaff and sit down, gazing in blank despair at the water. Is it possible? Is it not a hideous nightmare? But two minutes ago blessed beyond the lot of angling man — on the topmost pinnacle of angling fame! The practical possessor of the largest salmon ever taken with a rod! And now, deeper than ever plummet sounded, in the depths of dejection! Tears might relieve me; but my sorrow is too great, and I am doubtful how Ole might take it. I look at him again. The same utterly blank face, save a projection of unusual size in his cheek, which makes me conjecture that an additional quid has been secretly thrust in to supplement the one already in possession. He has said not a word since the catastrophe, but abundant expectoration testifies to the deep and tumultuous workings of his soul. I bear in mind that I am a man and a Christian, and I mutely offer him my flask. But, no; with a delicacy which does him honour, and touches me to the heart, he declines it, and with a deep sigh and in scarcely audible accents repeating — "The largest salmon I ever saw in my life!" — picks up my rod and prepares to depart. Why am I not a Stoic, and treat this incident with contempt? Yes, but why am I human? Do what I will, the vision is still before my eyes. I hear the "never, never" can the chance recur again! Shut my eyes, stop my ears as I will, it is the same.

If I had only known his actual weight! Had he but consented to be weighed and returned into the stream! How gladly would I now make that bargain with him! But the opportunity of even that compromise is past. It's intolerable. I don't believe the Stoics ever existed; if they did they must have suffered more than even I do in bottling up their miseries. They *did* feel; they *must* have felt — why pretend they didn't? Zeno was a humbug! Anyhow, none of the sect ever lost a salmon like that! What! "A small sorrow? Only a fish!" Ah, try it yourself! An old lady, inconsolable for the loss of her dog, was once referred for example of resignation to a mother who had lost her child, and she replied "Oh, yes! but *children are not dogs!*" And I, in some sort, understand her. So, in silent gloom I follow Ole homewards.

Not darkness, nor twilight, but the solemn yellow hues of northern midnight gather over the scene; black and forbidding frown the precipices on either side, save where on the top of the awful Horn — inaccessible as happiness — far, far beyond the reach of mortal footstep, still glows, like sacred fire, the sleepless sun! Hoarser murmurs seem to arise from the depths of the foss — like the groans of imprisoned demons — to which a slight but increasing wind stealing up the valley from the sea adds its melancholy note. My mind, already deeply depressed, yields helplessly to the influence of the hour and sinks to zero at once; and despondency — the hated spirit — descends from her "foggy cloud" and is my inseparable companion all the way home.

W. Bromley-Davenport
SALMON-FISHING
(Sport, London 1885).

THE FOLLOWING CHEFS HAVE CONTRIBUTED THEIR FAMOUS RECIPES:

Pierre Baran, Le Cirque,
New York, USA

Georges Blanc, Vonnas, France

Michel Blanchet, l'Ermitage,
Los Angeles, USA

J. Bowier, l'Aubergade,
Pontchartrain, France

Lothar Buck, Erbprinz,
Ettlingen, West Germany

Alain Chapel, Mionnay, France

Jacques Corbonnois,
Leves, France

Jean-Luc Danjou, Massy, France

Francis Dulucq, Sofitel Porticcio,
Porticcio, Corsica

Lennart Engström, Copenhague,
Paris, France

Gutbert Fallert, Talmühle,
Sasbachwalden, West Germany

Carlos Grootaert,
Auberge du Pré Bossu,
Moudeyres, France

Marc Haeberlin, Auberge de l'Ill,
Ribeauvillé, France

Eyvind Hellstrøm,
Bagatelle, Oslo, Norway

Peter G. Hinz, Haerlin,
Hamburg, West Germany

Ingrid Espelid Hovig,
The Norwegian Broadcasting
Corporation,
Oslo, Norway

Kenichi Judai, Hanagiri,
Osaka, Japan

Émile Jung, Au Crocodile,
Strasbourg, France

Wolf-Dieter Klunker,
Fischereihafenrestaurant,
Hamburg, West Germany

Louis Lachenal, Le Sauvage,
Rebais, France

Jacques Legrand, Rouvres, France

Jean-Louis Lieffroy, Falsled Kro,
Millinge, Denmark

Bernard Loiseau, La Côte-d'Or,
Saulieu, France

Manfred Mahnkopf, Grand Hôtel,
Stockholm, Sweden

Gualtiero Marchesi, Milano, Italy

Wolfgang Markloff, Erbprinz,
Ettlingen, West Germany

Steven Mellina,
The Manhattan Ocean Club,
New York, USA

Anton Mosimann, The Dorchester,
London, England

Walter Nichtawitz,
Lasse's Catering,
Brevik, Norway

Michael Oberleiter, La Fontaine,
Wolfsburg, West Germany

Louis Outhier, l'Oasis,
La Napoule, France

Andrew Pappas, The Post House,
New York, USA

Alain P. Sailhac, Le Cirque,
New York, USA

Harald Schultes, Neue Post,
Biessenhofen, West Germany

Hans Stucki, Stucki Bruderholz,
Basel, Switzerland

Werner Vögeli, Operakällaren,
Stockholm, Sweden

Eckart Witzigmann, Aubergine,
Munich, West Germany

Pierre Wynants, Comme Chez Soi,
Brussels, Belgium

Willy Wyssenbach, Continental,
Oslo, Norway

Today we can find fresh salmon on the menus of the better restaurants all over the world. This book contains salmon recipes from famous chefs from several corners of the world – besides the traditional specialities from Norway.

Salmon is a medium fat fish. The fish fat is valuable and important in a healthy diet, because it has poly-unsaturated fatty acids which lower the cholesterol content of the blood. Fish fat also contains the important vitamins A and D. Salmon can be served in many fashions – poached, fried or baked, cold and hot, smoked and marinated.

FRESH SALMON

Fresh salmon can be purchased in different states – in the round with head and innards, gutted (i.e. the belly is sliced open and the guts are removed), in slices, in fillets, etc.
The freshness of a salmon is recognized by:

a clean and fresh smell
bright, red gills
bright, protuding eyes
firm flesh
glossy, smooth skin

When the fish has scales, it should be scaled. In order to do this, use a knife or a scaler. Keep the knife lightly inclined so that it slips under the scales more easily. Salmon – which is to be poached or baked whole – or to be cut in slices – should be cleaned in the following fashion:
Place the salmon on its back. Make an incision around the vent and loosen the intestines. Loosen the gills and carefully pull out the guts. Take care not to puncture the gall bladder. The gall may give a bitter taste and an indelicate color to the fish. Cut off the head and the fins of the fish that is to be fried or baked whole. When liver, roe and soft roe are to be served, leave in cold water for an hour. Wash the fish under cold running water. Remove the blood along the backbone with a pointed knife and a small brush. Dry fish that is to be fried with a kitchen or paper towel. When the fish is to be filleted or poached, cut in pieces, it is cleaned as follows:

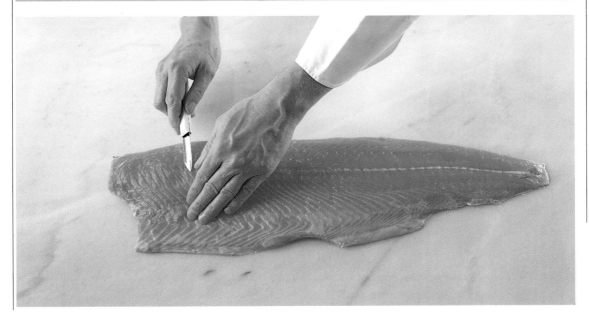

Place the fish on its back so that the innards fall back against the backbone. Slice open the belly with a knife or with scissors. Loosen the gills and pull out the guts. Take care not to puncture the gall bladder.

Rinse the fish thoroughly in cold running water. Remove the blood that is situated along the backbone at the same time.

If the fish is to be stuffed, it is practical to clean it from the back. Open the fish along the back and remove the guts that way.

With a sharp knife, loosen the backbone from the flesh, but cut the backbone at the head and the tail, so that the fish holds together.

Wash the fish.

DEEP-FREEZING

Salmon that is to be deep-frozen, should be frozen immediately after it has been cleaned and rinsed. This is very important to keep the quality. The best way is to water-glaze the fish. Place a cleaned and rinsed fish or a whole fish on a board and place it in the freezer.

After 24 hours take it out, dip it in cold water a couple of times. This prevents the air from coming into contact with the fish, and the salmon keeps much longer. Glazed fish is placed in plastic bags and returned to the freezer immediately. Fresh salmon that has been deep-frozen, may be kept in the freezer for 3 to 4 months.

Smoked salmon and gravlaks may be deep-frozen, provided it is well packed.

Cut the salmon in large pieces, sufficient for a one-time use and wrap the pieces individually in aluminum foil with an outer packing. Thaw overnight in refrigerator.

SMOKING SALMON

Salmon is well suited for smoking, and smoked salmon keeps longer. Besides, smoked salmon obtains a very good flavour and aroma as well as a delicate appearance. There are two variations of smoked salmon – warm-smoked and cold-smoked.

By warm-smoking, the fish is usually salted before it is dried and smoked at temperatures varying from 150° F to 185° F, depending on the size of the fish and the type of smoke chamber used. Salmon that is to be cold-smoked, is usually filleted. It is either placed in salt, or kept in a container with brine. Before it is to be smoked, it should be thoroughly dried. Cold-smoking takes place in smoke that varies from 70° F to 85° F, depending on the smoke chamber that is used.

When salting the fish, it should be kept in mind that a meager fish "takes salt" faster than a fat fish. Besides, a large fish needs more time for the salting and smoking processes.

PICKLED SALMON (CURING OF SALMON)

Pickled salmon is mostly used in the provinces (fylker) of Trønde-lag and further north in Norway.

Use the same type of fish as for preparing gravlaks (see page 32) – a fish of about 4 to 8 pounds. Clean, fillet and remove all the bones. Leave the skin on.

INGREDIENTS PER 2 POUNDS OF FISH:

2 1/3 ounces of salt
1 ounce of sugar
coarsely ground pepper

PREPARATION:

Rub the sugar and salt mixture on the flesh sides.
Sprinkle the pepper on top.
Place the fish with the skin down for 24 hours.
Turn over and place a lightly weighted board or similar on top for 2 days.
The pickled salmon should be ready after 3 days, however this depends somewhat on the size of the fish.
The pickled salmon is served with boiled potatoes, raw onion rings and sour cream.

CONVERSION TABLES

American measurements and terms have been used throughout this book. The following charts will be helpful in converting various weights, measurements, temperatures and terms.

LIQUID VOLUME

United States	U.K. Imperial	International (Metric)
1/2 teaspoon (tsp.)	1/2 tsp.	2.5 milliliters (ml.)
1 tsp.	1 tsp.	5 ml.
1 tablespoon (tbsp.) = 3 tsp.	1/2 fl. oz.	15 ml.
1 ounce (oz.) = 2 tbsp.	1 ounce	25 ml.
1/4 cup	2 fl. oz.	50 ml.
1/2 cup	4 fl. oz.	100 ml.
1 cup (c.) = 8 oz.	8 fl. oz.	225 ml.
1 pint (pt.) = 2 cups	16 fl. oz.	475 ml.
1 quart (qt.) = 2 pt.	1 1/2 pints	900 ml.
1 gallon (gal.) = 4 qt.	8 pints	4.5 litres

DRY VOLUME

United States	U.K. Imperial	International (Metric)
1 tablespoon	1/2 oz.	15 g.
1/4 cup	2 oz.	50 g.
1/2 cup	4 oz.	100 g.
1 cup	8 oz.	225 g.
2 cups	16 oz.	450 g.

LINEAR

For exact conversion use: 2.540005 x number of inches = centimeters

1/8 inch	= 0.3 centimeter		5 inches	=	12.5 centimeters
1/4 inch	= 0.5 centimeter		6 inches	=	15 centimeters
1 inch	= 2.5 centimeters		7 inches	=	17.5 centimeters
2 inches	= 5 centimeters		10 inches	=	25.5 centimeters
3 inches	= 7.5 centimeters		12 inches	=	30.5 centimeters

WEIGHT (AVOIRDUPOIS)

For quick conversions use: 25 grams = 1 ounce; 450 grams = 1 pound. Below are some exact equivalents. In recipes which require a fraction of an ounce (e.g., 1 2/3 ounces or 2 1/3 ounces) it is practical to either round the number up or down to the nearest full ounce. For example, 1 2/3 ounces could be 2 ounces; 3 1/3 ounces could be 3 ounces. The measurements should be converted to metric, accordingly.

1 ounce	= 25 grams	6 ounces	= 175 grams
2 ounces	= 50 grams	7 ounces	= 200 grams
3 ounces	= 75 grams	8 ounces	= 225 grams
4 ounces	= 100 grams	1 pound	= 450 grams
5 ounces	= 150 grams	2.2 pounds	= 1 kilogram

LIQUID AND DRY VOLUME TO U.K. IMPERIAL AND METRIC WEIGHT

1 generous cup of raw, medium-size shrimp	= 6 ounces	= 175 grams
1 generous cup of cooked baby shrimp	= 5 ounces	= 150 grams
1 cup of cooked, shredded crabmeat	= 7 1/2 ounces	= 215 grams
1 cup of raw fish fillets	= 6 ounces	= 175 grams
1 cup of *miso* (Japanese soybean paste)	= 9 ounces	= 250 grams
1 cup of bean curd, drained	= 4 ounces	= 100 grams
1 cup of all-purpose or whole-wheat flour	= 6 ounces	= 175 grams
1 cup of vegetable shortening	= 7 ounces	= 200 grams
1 cup of butter	= 8 ounces	= 225 grams
1 cup of whole, canned (tinned) tomatoes	= 7 1/2 ounces	= 213 grams
1 cup of fresh asparagus	= 4 ounces	= 100 grams
1 cup of fresh broccoli, sliced	= 4 ounces	= 100 grams
1 cup of granulated sugar	= 7 ounces	= 200 grams

TEMPERATURES

$$\text{Fahrenheit} = \frac{\text{Celsius x 9}}{5} + 32 \qquad \text{Celsius} = \frac{(\text{Fahrenheit} \cdot 32)}{9} \text{ x } 5$$

Oven Temperature Scales

Electric Scale ° Fahrenheit	° Celsius Scale	Gas Oven Marks
225° F	110° C	1/4
250	130	1/2
275	140	1
300	150	2
320/325	170	3
340/350	180	4
375	190	5
390/400	200	6
425/430	220	7
450	230	8
475/upwards	240	9

NOTE: The recipes in this book were written by individual chefs in the way that came most naturally to them. They are an expression of their flair in the kitchen, and, on occasion, presuppose a certain amount of knowledge.

For a glossary of terms, please see page 126.

SALAD FLORA DANICA

INGREDIENTS:

4 ounces of smoked salmon
  thinly sliced
8 ounces of smoked or cured
  halibut thinly sliced
2 ounces of celery root julienne
2 ounces of carrot julienne
2 ounces of apple julienne
2 ounces of raw champignon
  julienne
2 ounces of French string beans
1 small head of chicory
1 small head of lettuce
3 to 4 tablespoons of fresh or
  frozen lingonberries
1 tablespoon of olive oil
1 tablespoon of vinegar

INGREDIENTS FOR THE DRESSING:

1 tablespoon of French mustard
5 tablespoons of peanut oil
2 tablespoons of olive oil
sherry vinegar or similar
1 tablespoon of finely chopped
  fresh tarragon
salt and pepper

PREPARATION:

Cut the fish in julienne strips.
Steam the root celery and carrot
in a little butter under cover for
about 3 minutes. Place them
immediately in cold water with ice
cubes. Slice the string beans
lengthwise. Gently fry them in
butter and cool. The cooling
process makes the vegetables
keep their beautiful color.
The apple julienne stays in cold
water until the salad is to be set
up, otherwise it darkens.
Rinse thoroughly the lettuce and
the champignons. Dry and keep
the lettuce in a towel in the
refrigerator. Cut the champignons
in julienne strips.
All this can be prepared ahead of
time. Even the dressing can stay
in the refrigerator without
damage.
For the dressing: the oil is worked
into the mustard in trickles – like
when one makes mayonnaise.
The peanut oil has a very fine and
good taste, but the result is more
refined if one adds a little olive oil
– the proportions can vary
according to how "dramatic" the
olive oil tastes. Proceed by trying!
Add a little cold water to obtain
the right consistency.
Use the vinegar very carefully –
the acidity of the mustard may be
enough. Season with salt and
pepper, and add the tarragon.
Mix all the vegetables, the apple
and the lettuce well with the
dressing.

Arrange the salad as in the picture. Place the fish on top. At the last minute, heat some olive oil with a little vinegar in a frying pan and add the lingonberries. Shake the lingonberries until warm and sprinkle with a little vinegar.
Garnish each plate with the warm berries and serve.

Lennart Engström,
Copenhague,
Paris, France

SUMMER SALAD WITH SALMON

Serves: 4

INGREDIENTS:

4 portions of mixed greens for
  salad
1 ounce of lemon juice
1 ounce of olive oil
1 teaspoon of thin lemon peel
  strips, 1 inch long
1 ounce of butter
7 ounces of salmon, diced in
  1-inch cubes
salt, pepper and paprika
16 tops of chives
  (about 1 1/2 inches long)

PREPARATION:

Wash the greens and dry
thoroughly in towel or salad
basket. Blanch the lemon peel
and pour over a sieve. Heat the
butter in a pan, season the
salmon pieces with salt and
paprika, and fry carefully on all
sides, but let the insides be
slightly raw.

Lift the salmon pieces over on a
towel and keep warm.
Make the dressing with lemon
juice, oil, salt and pepper, and
mix in the strips of lemon peel,
and toss the salad with the
dressing. Arrange artfully on 4
plates and place the warm salmon
pieces on top. Decorate with the
chives.
Serve while the salmon is warm.

Willy Wyssenbach,
Continental,
Oslo, Norway

CHARLOTTE OF RAW SALMON WITH FENNEL ASPICS

(Charlotte de saumon cru aux aspics de fenouil)

Serves: 6

INGREDIENTS:

1 1/4 pounds of raw salmon
1 medium sized zucchini

Sauce:
1 generous cup of vinaigrette
1 egg yolk
1/2 avocado

Salt, pepper, green lemon, olive oil, green peppercorns, one cup of aspic jelly, one fennel, saffron, mustard.

PREPARATION:

Dice the raw salmon, season with salt, pepper, lemon juice, a dash of mustard, a dash of olive oil and a few crushed green peppercorns. Line the bottom and the sides of 6 ramekin moulds with slices of cooked and fluted zucchini. Garnish with the seasoned diced salmon. Refrigerate for 2 hours. Turn out on a dish.
Decorate with oak leaves and 2 aspics made from fish stock flavored with fennel and saffron. Pour the jelly into small barquettes.
Side dish: One half of an avocado with vinaigrette lightly thickened with egg yolk.

Émile Jung,
Au Crocodile,
Strasbourg, France

SPRING SALAD WITH SMOKED SALMON AND HALF COOKED EGG

Serves: 4

INGREDIENTS:

8 ounces of smoked salmon
4 medium sized eggs
sundry greens
8 Melba toasts

INGREDIENTS FOR THE DRESSING:

2 tablespoons of sherry vinegar
4 tablespoons of peanut oil or
 salad oil
1/2 teaspoon of salt
freshly ground white pepper

PREPARATION:

Select 4 to 5 fresh spring greens (spinach, chervil, cress, lettuce, radish etc.) and toss them in a light sherry vinaigrette dressing and arrange on a flat plate.
Boil the eggs for 5 minutes in salted boiling water, cool, peel and place them in the middle of the salad.
Cut the salmon julienne style, sprinkle over the salad. Just at the moment of serving, make a cut in the egg, in order to have the half cooked yolk flow out.
Serve with Melba toast.

Willy Wyssenbach,
Continental,
Oslo, Norway

SALAD ON GRAVLAKS OR SMOKED SALMON

Serves: 4

INGREDIENTS:

1 3/4 pounds of gravlaks or
 smoked salmon,
 diced in 1/2 inch cubes
12 fresh asparagus,
 white or green, cooked
4 freshly cooked artichoke
 hearts
16 leaves of fresh spinach,
 not blanched
1 to 4 heads of lettuce, chicory or
 Belgian endive
5 ounces of fresh chopped
 tomato
watercress
8 tails of crayfish
freshly ground pepper

GARNISH:

Mustard sauce with dill (see page 33), French baguette

PREPARATION:

1. Carefully wash the spinach, the chicory or the Belgian endive and arrange on a dish. Distribute the salmon cubes on the greens. Cut the asparagus in pieces, 1 or 2 inches long, dice or slice the artichoke hearts and arrange on the salmon, decorate with crayfish tails.
2. Spoon some mustard sauce with dill over it and sprinkle watercress and chopped tomato on top. Freshly ground pepper, if necessary.
Serve with fresh baguette, butter and mustard sauce with dill.

Walter Nichtawitz,
Lasse's Catering,
Brevik, Norway

ASPIC OF FRESH SALMON

Serves: 4

INGREDIENTS:

14 ounces of salmon fillet
1/2 quart of fish stock
1 2/3 ounces of carrots
1 2/3 ounces of green asparagus
1 2/3 ounces of zucchini
4 teaspoons of raspberry vinegar
4 teaspoons of red beet juice
1 cup of crème fraîche
6 leaves (1/2 ounce) of gelatine
salt and pepper

PREPARATION:

Blanch the salmon for 2 minutes. Cut the vegetables in julienne. Heat the fish stock, mix it with the red beet juice and the dissolved gelatine. Season well with the raspberry vinegar, salt and pepper.
Place the salmon and the vegetables in one aspic mould, or in 4 small ones, and fill the mould with the aspic mixture.
Let cool in the refrigerator for 12 hours.
Turn out the aspic on a dish, or on 4 plates, and serve with crème fraîche beside the aspic.

Harald Schultes,
Neue Post,
Biessenhofen, West Germany

SALMON MARINATED IN LEMON JUICE WITH QUAIL'S EGG AND HERB SAUCE

Serves: 4

INGREDIENTS:

14 ounces of salmon fillet
juice from 1 lemon
salt
freshly ground white pepper
1/2 tablespoon of thistle oil

SAUCE:

4 ounces of crème fraîche
2 2/3 ounces of yoghurt
1/3 ounce of parsley
1/3 ounce of dill ⎤
1/6 ounce of tarragon ⎟ finely chopped
1/6 ounce of chervil ⎦

Mix all the ingredients and season with salt and pepper.

PREPARATION:

Cut the salmon in thin slices. Mix the other ingredients well and brush over the slices. Let marinate for about 10 minutes.

GARNISH:

4 quails' eggs, poached

SERVING:

Mask the bottom of a plate with the sauce. Place the marinated slices of salmon on the sauce. Garnish with the poached quail's eggs and herbs.

Peter G. Hinz,
Haerlin,
Hamburg, West Germany

TERRINE OF SMOKED SALMON WITH VEGETABLES

Serves: 4

INGREDIENTS:

4 large slices of smoked salmon
1 tablespoon of butter
1/2 of a celery stalk
2 onions
1 red bell pepper
1 green bell pepper
2 carrots
2 ounces of French bread, diced
6 slices of pork fat
  (1/8 inch thick)
5 ounces of green beans
truffles and drained spinach
1 pint of milk
6 eggs
1/2 teaspoon of grated lemon
  rind
nutmeg, pepper and salt

GARNISH:

Sauce verte
toast

PREPARATION:

Dice the celery, onions, red and green bell peppers and carrots. Sweat the vegetables in butter carefully without giving color. Blend the bread cubes with the vegetables.
Line a cake pan with slices of pork fat. Fill half of the pan with the vegetable mixture and place a few green beans along the edge. Place the smoked salmon slices so they have the same length as the cake pan. Place the truffles and the spinach on the salmon and roll the slices to form a long cylinder.
Place the smoked salmon rolls in the middle of the cake pan. Fill the pan with the remaining vegetable mixture.

With a whisk, beat together the milk, eggs, a little salt, nutmeg and the grated lemon rind. Pour this into the pan. Place the remaining slices of pork fat on top, and poach the terrine in a bain marie (double-boiler) in a preheated oven at 212° F for 1 1/2 to 2 hours. When the dish is ready, it has the consistency of a pudding. Set aside and let cool overnight.
Before serving, dip the cake pan in water, turn it over to liberate the content. Cut in slices. Serve with sauce verte.

Walter Nichtawitz,
Lasse's Catering,
Brevik, Norway

BLINI WITH WHITE-FISH ROE AND SMOKED SALMON

Serves: 12

INGREDIENTS:

1/2 ounce of yeast
1 egg yolk
1 teaspoon of salt
3/4 cup of buck wheat
1/2 cup of wheat flour
1 cup of milk
1/2 cup of pilsner beer
1 egg white

GARNISH:

3 ounces of whitefish roe and julienne of smoked salmon
sour cream
chopped chives

PREPARATION:

Stir the yeast in a little milk, add the egg yolk, salt, flour and the remaining milk.
Stir until the mixture is even and smooth.
Add the beer. Cover the mixture and set aside to rise for about one hour.
When the mixture is ready, fold in the whipped egg white.
Fry the blinis on both sides on a slow fire until they are light brown. Place the blinis on a warm plate. Arrange the garnish on the side with a dab of sour cream and some chopped chives.
An exquisite hors d'oeuvre.

Walter Nichtawitz,
Lasse's Catering,
Brevik, Norway

FROZEN SALMON HORS D'OEUVRES FROM JAPAN

(Ruibe)

INGREDIENTS:

1 good-sized salmon fillet with a
 fine red color, skinned and
 boned
WASABI (green horseradish)
Soy sauce

PREPARATION:

Purchase a good fresh salmon of
fine color. Skin and bone, and
remove the small inner bones
with tweezers. Freeze the salmon
right away in the deep-freezer for
24 hours. Take the fish out and let
it thaw slowly, but it should still
be firm, so that it is easy to slice
into fine slices about 1/8 inch
thick.
The WASABI, which is a powder
made of green horseradish, is
stirred into the sauce. The thin
salmon slices are dipped into this
mixture.

Kenichi Judai,
Hanagiri
Osaka, Japan

POTTED SALMON TERRINE IN ENGLISH WINE JELLY

Serves: 10

INGREDIENTS:

2 pounds of fresh salmon
  (cut into thin escalopes)
6 fresh tomatoes
2 cooked carrots, cut lengthwise
2 ounces of spinach
4 ounces of broccoli
1 quart of fish aspic made with
  English white wine (Agdestone)
dill weed

INGREDIENTS FOR THE SAUCE:

English mustard
1/2 pint of mayonnaise
1/2 pint of cream
dill

METHOD:

Lightly poach the salmon escalopes in a little fish stock and white wine. Allow to cool.

PREPARE THE VEGETABLES:

a) Blanch and peel tomatoes.
b) Separate broccoli into florets.
c) Blanch spinach.
d) Cook carrots and cut lengthwise.

In a large terrine, apply a thin coat of fish aspic. Allow to set. Arrange alternate rows of vegetable (broccoli, carrots, spinach) in between the fresh salmon. When the terrine is full, gently pour in the prepared fish aspic, until it is level with the top of the terrine. Allow to set.

SERVING:

Place onto a plate with the sauce mayonnaise served in a sauce boat. Garnish accordingly.

Anton Mosimann,
The Dorchester,
London, England

SALMON SUSHI

INGREDIENTS:

1 fillet of good red salmon,
  skinned and boned
3 pounds of SUSHI rice
5 ounces of powder sugar
1 1/3 ounces of salt
4/5 cup of vinegar

PREPARATION:

Sprinkle the fillet with salt and
refrigerate for 8 to 12 hours.
Cook the rice, and when the rice
is ready and still warm, mix the
salt, sugar and vinegar thoroughly
and sprinkle over the rice. Set the
rice aside and let cool.
Wash the salmon briefly in
vinegar. Slice the salmon into
adequately big slices of about 1/8
inch thickness. Leave for a few
minutes. In an appropriate mould
(either in small individual ones,
or in a bigger one serving several
people), place one, or if
necessary several, slices of salmon
covering the bottom of the
mould.
Fill the mould with the rice and
press down very hard on the rice
with the lid. When the whole
SUSHI is firm, turn it out of the
form.

Kenichi Judai,
Hanagiri,
Osaka, Japan

COLD SALMON WITH FRESH ASPARAGUS

Serves: 4

INGREDIENTS:

1 1/2 to 2 pounds of fresh
  salmon, sliced
1 quart of water
1/2 cup of white wine
10 peppercorns
2 bay leaves
1 tablespoon of salt

GARNISH:

steamed potatoes
dill
creamed horseradish
15 shrimps
lemon sections
asparagus points

PREPARATION:

Bring to a boil the water, white
wine, peppercorns, bay leaves and
the salt. Place the slices of salmon
in the boiling liquid and let
simmer for about 15 minutes until
done. Leave the salmon in the
courtbouillon until the fish has
cooled down.
Take up the salmon slices, remove
the skin and the backbone. Place
the fish on a dish. Garnish with
the shrimps, the asparagus and
the lemon sections. Serve on the
side creamed horseradish and the
potatoes. Decorate with dill.
This dish can be served as an
hors d'oeuvre, but then the slices
must be divided in smaller
portions.

Walter Nichtawitz,
Lasse's Catering,
Brevik, Norway

SAVARIN OF SALMON WITH SHRIMPS AND TOMATOES

(Savarin de saumon et crevettes aux pommes d'amour)

Serves: 4

INGREDIENTS:

2 ounces of baby shrimps
1 ounce of butter
4 ounces of fresh salmon
2 ounces of Boston sole
1 egg
2 ounces of heavy cream
2 ounces of whipped cream
1 tablespoon of chopped parsley, chives and dill
1 tablespoon of chopped scallion
2 ounces of chopped black olives
2 ripe tomatoes
a few basil leaves
juice of half a lemon
2 tablespoons of olive oil

PREPARATION OF MOUSSE:

Sauté the shrimps for 20 seconds, add scallions, salt and pepper, and set aside to cool. Grind salmon and Boston sole in a blender for 30 seconds, add egg, and run again for 10 seconds. Add heavy cream, salt and pepper. Run again for 15 seconds. Place in a bowl and fold 2/3 of the shrimps with some lemon juice and whipped cream. Butter a 4-cup mould. Chop 1/3 of the shrimps, add the olives. Sprinkle into the mould. Fill the mould with the mousse. Place a buttered wax-paper on top and cook slowly for 30 minutes at 300 degrees F.

PREPARATION OF THE COULIS OF TOMATO:

Peel the tomatoes, discard the seeds, cut into large chunks. Process in a blender with lemon juice, olive oil, a few basil leaves. Add salt and pepper. Cut the savarin in 2 or 3 slices. Pour the coulis of tomato over the bottom of the dishes. Place the savarin on the coulis and decorate with basil leaves. Can be enjoyed hot or cold.

Alain P. Sailhac,
Le Cirque,
New York, USA

GRAVLAKS

Filleted salmon should be used for curing.

Clean the salmon thoroughly, removing all blood and the slime on the outside. Dry well with a kitchen towel or paper towel. Fillet the salmon. Ideal weight is 8 to 10 pounds, smaller fillets can also be used but then do not use the tail part. All the bones and fins must be removed. Keep the skin on.

GRAVLAKS WITH DILL

Per 2 pounds of salmon fillet:
2 tablespoons of sea salt or other salt without added chemicals
1 1/3 tablespoons of sugar
1 small teaspoon of freshly ground white pepper
1 handful of coarsely chopped dill with stems
4 teaspoons of dry sherry, or
4 teaspoons of brandy (these two items can be skipped)

Mix the salt, sugar and pepper and rub the meat sides of the fish with the mixture. Place one of the salmon sides, skin down, in an elongated plastic or steel container and sprinkle the dill over it. Moisten it with the brandy or the sherry and place the other side on top of it, with the skin up, but in the opposite direction, so that the thick dorsal side covers the thinner ventral side. One can also sprinkle some dill stems on top. Place the salmon in a cool (40 to 50 degrees F) location for 2 days. Turn the sides around 4 times during these days and baste with the brine that is formed. The salmon may remain longer, but after 4 to 5 days it begins to be stiff and hard, loses its fine consistency and appears to be dry.

Cut the salmon slantingly in thin slices, decorate with some leaves of crisp lettuce and some sprigs of dill.

Serve with toast and butter or a French baguette. In Scandinavia it is often served with creamed potatoes to which is added a little chives and plenty of mustard sauce.

MUSTARD SAUCE FOR GRAVLAKS:

2 tablespoons of good French mustard
1/3 tablespoon of Colman's Dry Mustard
1/2 egg yolk
1 teaspoon of sugar
juice of 1/4 lemon
1/2 cup of oil
2 tablespoons of chopped dill

Dissolve the Colman's Mustard in the lemon juice, combine the two mustards, the sugar and the egg yolk in a small bowl or a deep plate. Add the oil a little at a time, and last, add the dill.
Season to taste.

GRAVLAKS WITH TARRAGON

Use the same recipe as for *Gravlaks with dill,* the tarragon replacing the dill both on the fish and in the mustard sauce.

GRAVLAKS WITH RED PEPPER

Per 2 pounds of salmon fillet:
2 tablespoons of sea salt
1 tablespoon of sugar
2 tablespoons of ground red pepper
1 ounce of dry sherry

The salmon should marinate for 2 days. Before it is sliced, scrape away the pepper, add 1/3 of it to the mustard sauce.

GRAVLAKS WITH LEMON

Per 2 pounds of salmon fillet:
2 tablespoons of sea salt
2/3 ounce of sugar
1 small teaspoon of freshly ground white pepper
1/2 tablespoon of crushed mustard seeds
1 ounce of lemon juice
1 ounce of sherry

Cut the salmon in thin slices and place them on a plastic or a stainless steel tray. Spread the mixture of salt, sugar and the spices on the slices and moisten with lemon juice and sherry. Place the salmon in a cool location for 6 hours and turn the slices once.

Ingredients for the sauce:

1 tablespoon of French mustard
2 tablespoons of French mustard with mustard seeds, old style
1/2 egg yolk
juice of 1/2 lemon
1/2 cup of oil
salt and pepper

Willy Wyssenbach,
Continental,
Oslo, Norway

GRAVLAKS WITH SPRING ONION STEWED IN CREAM AND MUSTARD

Serves: 4

INGREDIENTS:

13 ounces of gravlaks, sliced
7 ounces of spring onions, sliced in 2-inch long parts (use lower part of the vegetable)
1 pint of heavy cream
1 tablespoon of mustard (French type)
salt

DECORATION:

fresh lettuce leaves

PREPARATION:

Blanch the spring onions in salted boiling water. Pour into a colander and transfer to ice cold water. Strain and dry in a kitchen towel. Reduce the heavy cream in a saucepan, stirring with a wooden spatula so the cream does not stick to the pan. Add the mustard, the spring onions and season with salt.

Arrange the salmon slices on a plate with the warm creamed onions. Decorate with some lettuce and serve with bread.

Willy Wyssenbach,
Continental,
Oslo, Norway

COLD MOUSSE OF GRAVLAKS

Serves: 4

INGREDIENTS:

10 ounces of gravlaks,
  diced for the processor
4 ounces of gravlaks,
  sliced for decoration
4 tablespoons of sour cream
  20% fat
1 tablespoon mustard sauce
lettuce leaves for decoration
dill for decoration

May be served on:
1. whole wheat bread
2. avocado halves, sprinkled with
lemon juice
3. halves of boiled eggs
(boiled 8 min.)
4. small French bread croutons for
snacks

PREPARATION:

Prepare the mousse in food
processor or chop finely with
knife. Place fish in processor, add
an ice cube, run a few seconds,
add sour cream, mustard sauce
and run a few seconds longer.

MUSTARD SAUCE FOR GRAVLAKS:

2 tablespoons of good French
  mustard
1/3 tablespoon of Colman's Dry
  Mustard
1/2 egg yolk
1 teaspoon of sugar
juice of 1/4 lemon
1/2 cup of oil
2 tablespoons of chopped dill

Dissolve the Colman's Mustard in
the lemon juice, combine the two
mustards, the sugar and the egg
yolk in a small bowl or a deep
plate. Add the oil a little at a time,
and last, add the dill.

Willy Wyssenbach,
Continental,
Oslo, Norway

COLD MOUSSE OF SALMON WITH TOMATO SAUCE

Serves: 10

INGREDIENTS:

3 ounces of smoked salmon,
  lightly sauteed
3 1/2 ounces of poached fresh
  salmon
3 ounces of fish veloute made
  from bones and trimmings
  of sole
1 leaf gelatine about 1/10 ounce
1 cup of heavy cream,
  lightly beaten
3/4 ounce of Cognac
3/4 ounce of white wine
salt and white pepper (from mill)
fresh smoked salmon and salmon
  roe as garnish.

PREPARATION:

Process the smoked salmon, the
poached salmon and the fish
veloute in a blender and strain it
through a fine sieve. The leaf
gelatine is soaked and melted in
the white wine. Let it cool and
mix it with the salmon mousse.
Carefully fold in the lightly beaten
cream. Season with Cognac, salt
and white pepper.
Pour into moulds and place it in a
cold place for about 8 hours. Turn
out the mousse. Garnish with
slice of smoked salmon cut to
size and top with salmon roe and
a sprig of dill.

SAUCE MADE FROM FRESH TOMATOES:

Peel 8 fresh tomatoes and sqeeze
out the seeds. Process in blender
but not too fine, add a little salt,
white pepper, sugar, olive oil and
red wine vinegar.
Serve the mousse on a plate with
the tomato sauce around it.

Manfred Mahnkopf,
Grand Hôtel,
Stockholm, Sweden

GRAVLAKS MOUSSE

Serves: 6

INGREDIENTS:

1 pound 5 ounces mousse of
  gravlaks (see page 33)
6 sheets (1/2 ounce) of gelatine
12 slices of gravlaks
18 small gherkins (cornichons)
1 1/4 cups of mustard sauce
  (see page 33)
1/4 cup of light stock

PREPARATION:

Soak the sheets of gelatine in cold
water for a few minutes. Heat the
stock and dissolve the gelatine.
When dissolved, quickly mix in
the mousse.
Rinse a pie form in cold water
and without drying it, fill it with
the mousse and set aside in the
refrigerator for a few hours.
Arrange the mousse on a plate
with the slices of gravlaks around
it. Mix the gherkins in the
mustard sauce and serve on the
side.

Willy Wyssenbach,
Continental,
Oslo, Norway

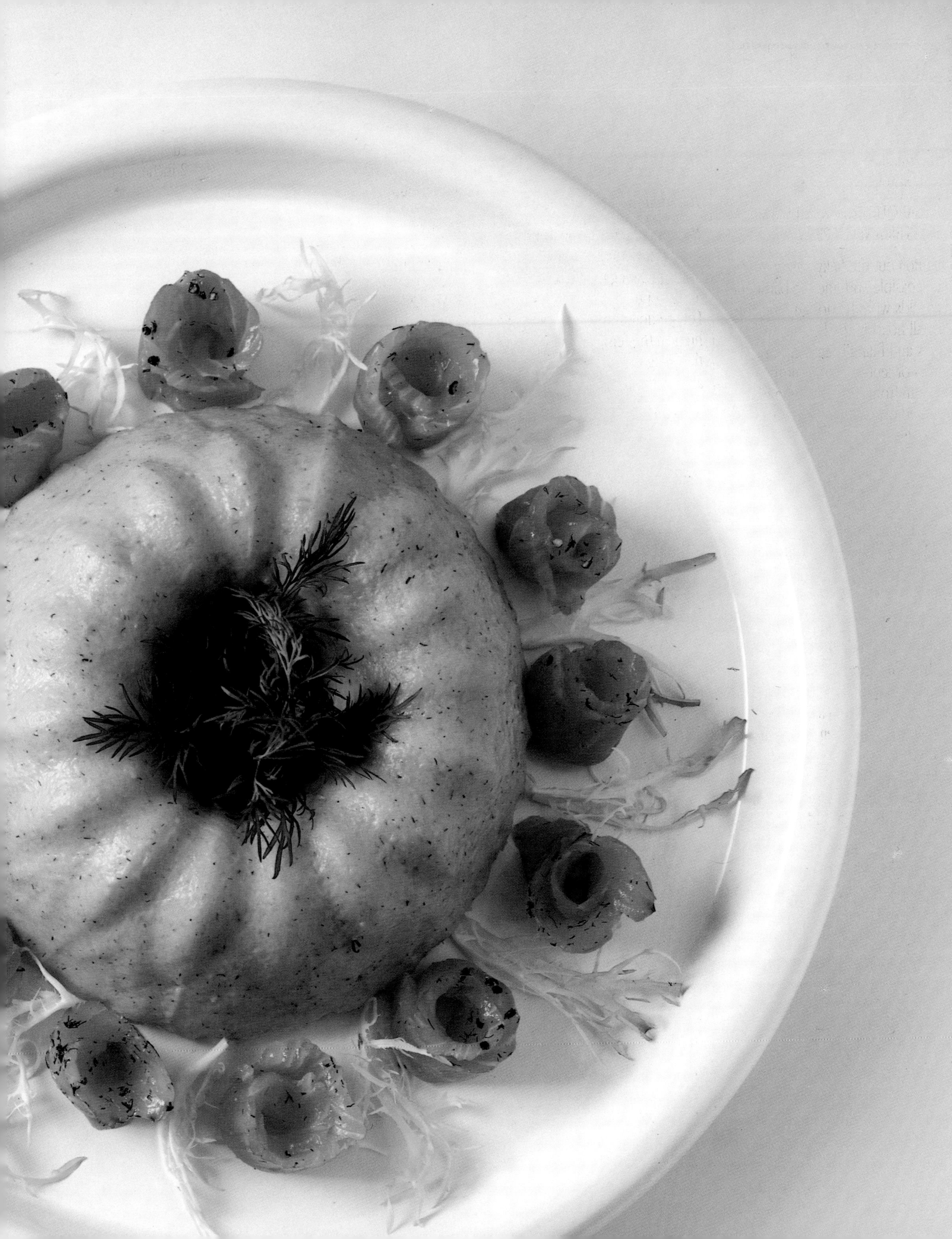

SALMON SNACKS

1. FRESHLY BAKED CREAM PUFF PASTRIES FILLED WITH MOUSSE OF GRAVLAKS

Force the mousse from a bag through the side or the bottom of the pastries.

2. BARQUETTES WITH SALMON BUTTER AND CAPERS

a) Roll out the flaky pastry as thin as possible and line the barquette moulds with the dough, pricking small holes in the bottom with a fork and filling them with dried peas or lentils to prevent the dough from rising. Bake in a pre-heated oven at 350° F for 15 to 18 minutes.
b) Salmon butter: 3 1/3 ounces of butter and 2 ounces of pureed smoked salmon are beaten well together and mixed with capers.

3. SALMON TARTARE ON WHOLE WHEAT BREAD WITH SALMON ROE

Ingredients:
3 1/3 ounces of coarsely chopped
  boned fresh salmon
1/2 crushed anchovy fillet
1/2 finely chopped shallot
1 tablespoon of crème fraîche
5 drops of Cognac
1 teaspoon of parsley greens
1 2/3 ounces of salmon roe
salt and freshly ground pepper
watercress and chervil for
  decoration

Preparation:

Mix all the ingredients and season with salt and pepper. Decorate with watercress and chervil.

4. SALMON BISCUITS

Ingredients:

7 ounces of sifted flour
4 ounces of butter
5 ounces of puréed smoked
  salmon
1 egg yolk
1 tablespoon of water,
  (if necessary)

Preparation:

Mix the butter and the flour on the table, adding the smoked salmon, the egg yolk, some salt and pepper.
Let the dough rest for at least one hour in the refrigerator. Roll out the dough to about 1/8 of an inch and prick the surface. Cut out the dough to biscuit shapes and bake on baking paper in a preheated oven at 390° F for 18 to 20 minutes.

5. FLAKY PASTRY STICKS WITH SMOKED SALMON

Ingredients:

3 1/3 ounces of flaky pastry
  dough
1 2/3 ounces of smoked salmon in
  thin strips
paprika powder
1 egg

Preparation:

Roll the flaky pastry dough to about 1/8 of an inch thickness. Cut the dough in strips about 1/2 inch wide and 3 inches long. Distribute the salmon evenly on the strips and place these on a baking paper and brush over with a beaten mixture of the egg and some water. Place the paper with the strips on a baking sheet in a preheated oven at 340° F for 15 minutes. Push the strips (sticks) together and sprinkle with paprika powder.

6. SALMON CANAPÉS

Toast some slices of brioche, cover with slices of smoked salmon.
Cut out canapés as triangles or squares and decorate with a small salmon rosette.

7. POCKETS OF FLAKY PASTRY FILLED WITH CREAMED SALMON AND SORREL

Ingredients:

3 1/3 ounces of flaky pastry rolled
  out to 1/8 inch thickness
1 whole egg
1 cup of reduced heavy cream
1 handfull of sorrel julienne
1 2/3 ounces of finely diced
  smoked salmon
salt and pepper

Preparation:

Half of the pastry dough is divided into small squares, 3/4 by 3/4 inch. Place these on a baking sheet covered with baking paper. Brush the squares with the beaten egg. In the middle of the squares place a small quantity of a mixture consisting of the salmon and the sorrel in the heavy cream.
The other half of the pastry sheet is divided into squares measuring 1 x 1 inch which are placed on top of the creamed fillings. The edges are pressed together with a ruler or a pencil. Brush the top with egg and set aside in the refrigerator for 20 minutes.
In a preheated oven at 390° F bake for about 20 minutes.

8. MOUSSE OF GRAVLAKS ON CROUTONS

Ingredients:

2 1/2 ounces of gravlaks, sliced
2 1/2 ounces of mousse of
  gravlaks (see page 33)
slices of white crustless bread,
  cut into 10 round canapés,
  2 inches in diameter
1 2/3 ounces of clarified butter
dill

Preparation:

Fry the canapés in butter to golden brown.
Set aside on paper
or kitchen towel to drain excess butter.
Through a bag force a ring of mousse on the edges of the canapés. Cut the gravlaks slices in strips a little under 1 inch wide.
Roll these together, place them standing in the middle of the croutons and decorate with dill.

Willy Wyssenbach,
Continental,
Oslo, Norway

SALMON TARTARE

(Tartare de saumon)

Serves: 6

INGREDIENTS:

1 pound of fillet of salmon
6 tails of Dublin Bay prawns
6 fillets of anchovy
3 egg yolks
2 tablespoons of green pepper
2 tablespoons of chopped parsley
2 sweet and sour pickles
12 capers
8 tablespoons of olive oil (virgin)
1 dash of Worcester sauce
3 drops of Tabasco sauce
1 teaspoon of sherry vinegar
1 teaspoon of Cognac
1 tablespoon of carrot stock

Chop the salmon meat, the prawns and the anchovy with a knife rather finely. Chop all the spices and herbs finely. Add the egg yolks, salt, then vinegar, as well as the carrot stock and the olive oil. Last, add Cognac, Worcester and Tabasco. Make small patties of the salmon.

INGREDIENTS FOR DECORATION:

Julienne of carrots
butter
1 large tomato
small sprigs of fresh chervil

PREPARATION FOR DECORATION:

Lightly cook the carrots in a little water and butter. Peel and dice the tomato.

*Lennart Engström,
Copenhague,
Paris, France*

TERRINE OF SMOKED SALMON MOUSSE

(Mousse de saumon fumé en terrine)

INGREDIENTS:

8 ounces of fresh salmon
  (skinned and cut in small strips)
olive oil
8 ounces of smoked salmon,
  sliced
1 dash of Cognac
1 tablespoon of fresh
  peppercorns
1 pint of heavy cream
1 pinch of freshly ground pepper

PREPARATION:

Saute the fresh salmon in olive oil on low heat. Cook while stirring with a spatula. Flambé with Cognac. Refrigerate.
Process the smoked salmon in a blender with half of the heavy cream until smooth. Mix in the cooked fresh salmon. Add peppercorns and the remainder of the heavy cream.
Cool and serve.

Pierre Baran,
Le Cirque,
New York, USA

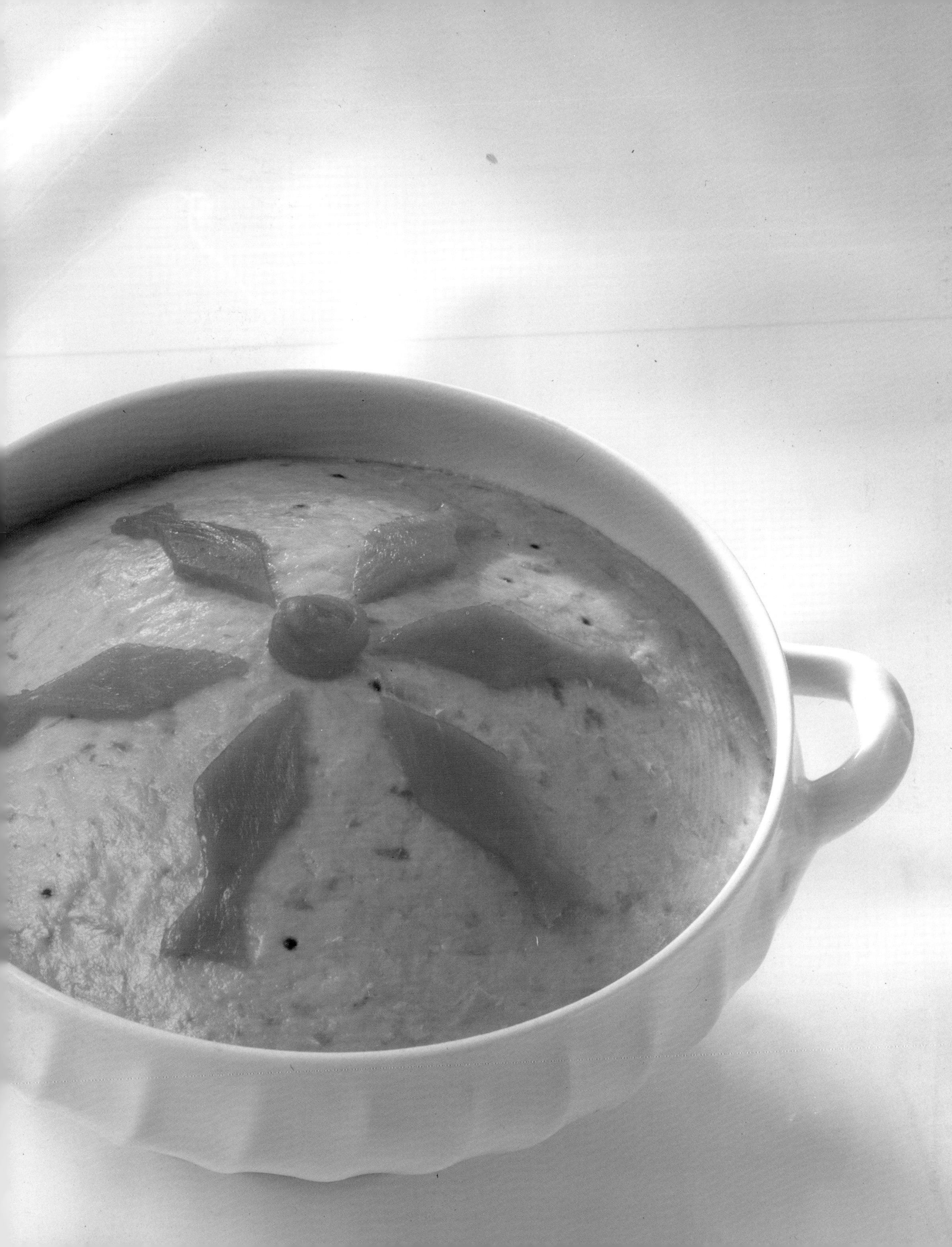

Salmon

TRUFFLED SALMON WITH SMALL SALAD

(Truffade de saumon, petite salade.)

Serves: 4

INGREDIENTS:

1/2 teaspoon of good gelatine
1/2 cup of milk
1 ounce of butter
1 ounce of flour
3 ounces of green asparagus or
   asparagus points
7 ounces of fresh salmon meat
3 1/2 ounces of smoked salmon
1 large egg
2 teaspoons of truffle juice
1/2 cup of good crème fraîche
1/3 ounce of truffle or truffle
   peels
salt, freshly ground pepper
Cayenne pepper

PREPARATION:

(cooking time: 1 to 1 1/4 hours)
1. Moisten the gelatine in cold water for 5 minutes.
2. Prepare a panada as follows: boil the milk with 1/2 ounce of butter, add the drained gelatine and let melt. Remove from fire

and add the flour, mix well. Beat briskly with a wooden spatula on a brisk fire until the mixture practically does not stick to the pan or the spatula. Remove and place the panada on a plate and let cool.

3. Cut 1 inch of the asparagus. Wash the points and cook in salted water. Keep them lightly crisp and set aside to cool.

4. Work the two types of salmon in a processor until very fine. Add the panada and run the processor for another minute. Add the egg and process a little longer. Add the truffle juice and work the panada through a fine sieve with a plastic or stainless steel spoon.

5. Place this mixture (4.) in a large bowl. Place this bowl in a larger bowl half filled with crushed ice. With a wooden

spatula work the mixture, adding the crème fraîche a little at a time. This procedure should be done on ice in order to give the mixture body.

6. Chop the truffles rather finely.

7. Season the mixture with salt, pepper and Cayenne pepper. Add and mix in the chopped truffles.

8. Dry the asparagus on a towel.

9. Butter the entire inside of a baking dish, 2 1/4 x 3 x 9 inches.

10. Place half of the truffled mixture (7.) in the dish, arranging on top the asparagus lengthwise and covering the mixture completely. Fill the dish with the remaining mixture. Check that the dish is completely filled and even.

11. Butter one side of a piece of aluminum foil and place that side on the dish.

12. Place the dish in a shallow pan half filled with water. Bring the water to a boil and place in a preheated oven, 350° F, for 1 1/4 hours.

13. Remove the dish from the pan, let cool and place in the refrigerator for at least 24 hours.

SERVING:

14. Cut into even slices. Serve at room temperature, with a small salad.

Pierre Wynants,
"Comme chez soi",
Brussels, Belgium

WEST COAST SALMON SOUP WITH QUENELLES AND PURSLANE

Serves: 6

INGREDIENTS FOR THE SOUP:

1 2/3 ounces of butter
1 2/3 ounces of flour
1 1/2 quarts of salmon and fish stock
1/2 cup of sour cream
1 egg yolk
salt and pepper

INGREDIENTS FOR THE QUENELLES OF SALMON:

1/2 pound of finely ground salmon (rub the fish through a fine sieve)
3 egg whites (from medium-sized eggs)
1/4 cup of heavy cream
salt and pepper

INGREDIENTS FOR PICKLED PURSLANE:

(should marinate for 1 to 2 days)
3 1/3 ounces of purslane stems
3 1/3 ounces of sugar
1/4 cup of vinegar (5%)
cinnamon
1 clove

PREPARATION OF THE SALMON SOUP:

Melt the butter in a heavy saucepan, add the flour and stir until smooth. Set the saucepan aside, let the mixture cool and then pour the scalding stock over it and bring it all to boil while constantly stirring with a whisk. Let the soup cook over a slow fire for about an hour, stir a few times with a wooden spoon, and skim. Set the saucepan aside. Mix the sour cream and the egg yolk well and pour the soup over it while briskly stirring with a whisk. Strain the soup through a fine sieve or a cloth and keep covered and warm.

PREPARATION OF THE SALMON QUENELLES:

Chill the salmon and place in a cold bowl (if possible place the bowl in a larger one with some crushed ice). Mix the egg whites, one at a time, with the salmon, add the heavy cream, a little at a time, while stirring evenly with a wooden spoon. Season with salt and pepper. Let the mixture rest for a few minutes. Bring the lightly salted fish stock to a boil. Make small quenelles of the salmon mixture and let them draw in the fish stock for 4 to 5 minutes.

PREPARATION OF THE PICKLED PURSLANE:

Remove the leaves and the branches from the purslane. Wash the stems, cut them in pieces, about 2 inches long, and fasten them together with a string. Place the bundles in lightly salted boiling water and let them cook over a moderate fire until tender. Quickly chill and dry them on a towel.
Bring the vinegar with the sugar, cinnamon and clove to a boil. Cool and pour over the purslane either in a jar or a ceramic bowl. Cut the purslane julienne style or round slices and serve with the soup.

Willy Wyssenbach,
Continental,
Oslo, Norway

RUSSIAN SALMON SOUP

This is originally a Russian soup. The innumerable variations we may encounter, all pretend to be the only genuine recipe, but the genuine Russian salmon soup must contain fermented cabbage, pickled gherkins and "smetana".

Serves: 4

INGREDIENTS:

1 pound of salmon
1 1/4 quarts of fish stock
1 onion
1 leek
1 sprig of parsley
1 carrot
1 piece of celeriac, about 3 1/3 ounces
2 to 3 potatoes
2 tablespoons of butter or margarine
1/2 teaspoon of thyme
1 bay leaf
2 tablespoons of tomato puree
1/4 to 1/2 cup of chopped parsley
1 tablespoon of capers
1/2 pickled gherkin, sliced

IN THE SOUP:

1 to 1 1/2 cups of "smetana" or sour cream

PREPARATION:

Clean and rinse the fish. Cut the boned and skinned salmon in fillets. Make a good fish stock of the trimmings and the head. Add the onion, the green parts of the leek and the parsley sprig to the stock and let simmer for 20 to 30 minutes. Strain the stock.

Clean the carrot and the celeriac. Peel the potatoes. The potatoes give the soup body. Cut the carrot and the celeriac in julienne, cut the white part of the leek in fine slices, and dice the potatoes. Sweat all these vegetables in a little butter or margarine on a brisk fire for a few minutes. Add the fish stock. Add the thyme and the bay leaf, and let the soup simmer for about 10 minutes under cover. Dice the boned and skinned salmon into large cubes.

Remove the bay leaf and add the tomato puree and the salmon cubes.
Let the soup simmer for another 15 minutes.
Add parsley, capers and the gherkin slices. Season to taste. The thyme may be replaced by a crushed clove of garlic.
Serve the soup with "smetana" or sour cream, also with more capers and gherkins, if desired.
Serve with a baguette or some French rolls.

Ingrid Espelid Hovig,
The Norwegian Broadcasting
Corporation,
Oslo, Norway

SALMON HOT POT

(Ishikari-nabe)

The most well-known NABE-MONO (hot pot) in Hokkaido. It is cooked in an earthenware pot called DONABE, and people cook and eat together around the table. It is essentially a winter-dish.

Serves: 4

INGREDIENTS:

1 pound 5 ounces of salmon
1 quart 7 ounces of vegetable
  stock (or water)
KOMBU (dried seaweed)
KATSUO (dried bonito shavings)
10 ounces of white MISO
  (bean paste)
2 ounces of white radish
  (8 pieces)
1 1/3 ounces of carrots (4 pieces)
2 1/3 ounces of SHIITAKE
  mushrooms (4 pieces)
13 ounces of Chinese cabbage
  (4 pieces)
3 1/3 ounces of KIKUNA
  (kind of chrysanthemum leaves)
2 2/3 ounces of leeks
  (or green onions)
1 1/2 blocks of TOFU
  (bean curd)
salt

PREPARATION:

Scale and bone the salmon. Reserve the guts and the bones. It should be pointed out that under more formal occasions, the guts and bones can be left out of the dish. Chop the salmon as well as the bones and the guts into chunks. Sprinkle with salt.

Prepare a fish stock from the vegetable "bouillon", the KOMBU and the KATSUO. Mix the MISO into the stock.
When the stock is ready, place the salmon and trimmings in the stock and simmer until the fish is ready, but still firm. Put the pre-cut vegetables into the pot and simmer carefully for a little longer. Add the diced TOFU. At this point the cooking should stop. The pot is prepared and served at the table. Each guest helps himself from the pot, and as the pot is being emptied, new ingredients are added.

Kenichi Judai,
Hanagiri,
Osaka, Japan

FRESH SALMON WITH CITRONELLA

(Saumon frais à la citronelle)

Serves. 6

INGREDIENTS:

1 salmon, good 4 pounds
1 pike, good 2 pounds
2 to 3 whiting, one pound each
18 crayfish
1 1/2 pounds of cèpes (boletus)
11 ounces of butter
champagne
1 quart of dry white wine
1 pound of medium-sized
  champignons
2/3 quart of cream
1 1/2 lemons
1 1/2 limes
leaves of citronella

PREPARATION:

Gut the salmon through the belly and remove all bones.
Gut the pike and the whiting. Using the bones, make a good fish stock.
Gut the crayfish, then cook à la Bordelaise. Shell the tails, but reserve the bodies.
Stuff the salmon with a mousse made of 3/4 pike and 1/4 whiting, to which has been added a julienne of cèpes à la Bordelaise and a few slices of crayfish tails. Reserve a little of this mousse to garnish the crayfish bodies.
In a saumonière heat some butter. Place the salmon on its belly and sauté lightly. Moisten with a good champagne and cook over slow fire, basting frequently.
When the fish is done, skin the salmon carefully, removing the dorsal fin and concealing the aperture with trimmed champignons.
Set aside, covered with a moist cloth, keep warm.
Strain the cooking liquid, reducing to 1/4 of its volume. Add 2/3 quart of cream. Reduce once more in bain-marie. Add the juice of the lemon and the lime. Shred some of the rind of the lemon and the lime into the sauce. Add a little butter before serving and sprinkle with chopped citronella leaves.

SERVING:

Mask a heavy serving dish with hot sauce.
Place the salmon on its belly.
Decorate with crayfish bodies.
Serve the remaining sauce on the side in a sauce boat.

Francis Dulucq,
Sofitel Porticcio,
Porticcio, Corsica

BRAISED SALMON WITH LARDOONS AND CIDER

(Saumon rôti aux lardons à la lie de cidre)

Serves: 6

GENERAL INGREDIENTS:

2/3 quart of heavy crème fraîche
1 pound 5 ounces of butter
salt
freshly ground white pepper
paprika

INGREDIENTS FOR THE FISH:

1 salmon of 4 pounds
11 ounces of salt pork
3/4 of a leek
1 carrot
1 stalk of celery
1 shallot
thyme, bay leaf and chervil
2 ounces of champignons
6 crayfish
1 cup of dry cider

INGREDIENTS FOR THE STOCK:

Bones of 1 1/2 sole and
  1/2 turbot
1/2 onion
1 sprig of parsley and of chervil
1 glass of dry white wine
1/4 of a lemon
1 ounce of stems of champignon

PREPARATION:

1) Take the salmon, open it by the belly, removing all the bones but leave the backbone. Trim it, removing fins, scales etc., but leave the head and the tail, which will allow it to stand up. Season with salt, pepper and paprika. Lard the two fillets with small lardoons which have been blanched beforehand.

2) Butter a pan large enough for the salmon. Place the crushed bones of the fish and a fine julienne of vegetables: carrot, white parts of the leek, the celery, the shallot. Add the bay leaf, thyme, chervil, stems of champignons. Sweat.
Moisten with 1 cup of dry cider and 1 cup of fish stock.
Place the salmon in the pan. Brush with butter before it goes into a medium hot oven. Cook slowly for about 30 minutes, basting frequently.
When the fish is ready, drain off excessive liquid. Keep warm.

PREPARATION OF THE SAUCE:

Reduce the cooking liquid, the fish stock, and strain through a fine sieve. Add the cream and work in the butter.

1. GARNISH:

Crayfish Thermidor
Crayfish tails in flaky pastry

7 ounces of flour
1 ounce of Maizena (corn starch)
3 ounces of margarine or butter
32 crayfish of which 6 very large
1/2 ounce of Parmesan
2 cups of dry white wine
2/3 liqueur glass of Cognac
2/3 tablespoon of tomato paste
2/3 tablespoon of hot mustard
2/3 tablespoon of chopped
  parsley
2 shallots

Crayfish Thermidor

Remove the shells from the crayfish tails and slice the crayfish lengthwise. Roast, then cut in slices and mask with reduced Bercy sauce flavored with mustard, and mixed with Mornay sauce. Glaze.

Crayfish Tails in Flaky Pastry

Make 6 small flaky pastries. Once baked, open and place 4 to 5 crayfish in each pastry (these tails will have been treated à la Bordelaise). Mask.

2. GARNISH:

Small bunches of asparagus spears with morels on artichoke hearts.

6 artichokes
18 small asparagus
1 fresh morel

Garnish the artichoke hearts with a small bunch of asparagus spears. Mask with cream sauce. Decorate with slices of morels. Glaze. (It is understood that the artichoke hearts, the asparagus and the morels have been treated beforehand.)

SERVING:

Place the salmon on its belly in the middle of the serving dish. Decorate with 6 trussed crayfish. Alternate the garnishes around the fish.
Lightly mask with the sauce.
Serve sauce on the side in a sauce boat.

Louis Lachenal,
Le Sauvage,
Rebais, France

BRAISED FILLET OF SALMON IN DILL WITH WHITEFISH CAVIAR

(Supreme de saumon dans sa nage à l'aneth au caviar rouge du pays)

Serves: 4

INGREDIENTS:

1 pound 5 ounces of boned and
  skinned fillet of salmon,
  in 4 slices
3 1/3 ounces of butter
1 tablespoon of finely chopped
  shallot
1 cup of fish stock
1 cup of dry white wine
1/2 lemon
1 cup of heavy cream
2 tablespoons of coarsely
  chopped dill
1 small leek, cut julienne style
1 piece of celeriac,
  cut julienne style
1 small carrot, cut julienne style
flaky pastry
4 teaspoons of whitefish roe
salt and pepper

PREPARATION:

Butter a pan with 2 teaspoons of butter. Spread the shallot on the bottom. Place the salmon in the pan, season with salt and pepper. Add the fish stock (see below) and the white wine. Squeeze the juice of 1/2 a lemon in the stock and cover with a buttered paper. Bring to a boil and let simmer for 5 minutes. Remove the fish and set aside. Keep warm.
Strain the stock into another saucepan, add the cream, and reduce to 1/3 of the volume, i.e. about 1 cup. Finish the sauce by working in 2 ounces of the butter. Add the dill. Correct the seasoning with salt, pepper and lemon juice.
Sauté the vegetables in 2/3 ounce of butter and let simmer for 5 minutes without coloring. Season with salt and pepper. The julienne should still be crisp.
Place the salmon on warm plates, distribute the sauce on top of the fish and garnish with the vegetables. Place the bouché filled with the whitefish roe next to the salmon.

INGREDIENTS FOR
THE FISH STOCK:

Bones, trimmings and head of the
  salmon
1/2 of a yellow onion
green parts of a leek, sliced
parsley stems
1 sprig of thyme
white peppercorns

PREPARATION OF
THE FISH STOCK:

Thoroughly rinse the bones and trimmings in cold running water. Place in a saucepan, add water to cover the bones. Add the other ingredients and boil slowly for about 15 minutes. Skim a few times and strain through a cloth.

PREPARATION FOR
THE BOUCHE:

Roll out the flaky pastry dough to 1/8 inch thickness. Cut out circles 1 1/4 inches in diameter. Out of a 1/4 inch thick dough make rings with an inner diameter of one inch. Place the rings on top of the circles. Bake in a preheated oven at 410 to 430° F for 10 minutes.

Werner Vögeli,
Operakällaren,
Stockholm, Sweden

BRAISED SALMON WITH CHAMPAGNE

(Saumon braisé au champagne)

Serves: 8 to 10

INGREDIENTS:

1 salmon of 5 1/4 pounds
onion rings
parsley stems
2 sprigs of thyme
1 bay leaf
salt and pepper
3/4 bottle of Champagne Brut
fish stock (see below)

PREPARATION OF SALMON:

Place the salmon with onion rings, parsley stems, 2 sprigs of thyme, one bay leaf, salt and pepper and 3/4 of a bottle of Champagne Brut in a fish kettle. Add fish stock so the liquid half covers the fish. Bring to a boil, then place in an oven for 20 minutes. Baste from time to time to keep the fish moist. Cover the kettle with an aluminum foil. Set aside, but keep warm.

INGREDIENTS FOR FISH STOCK:

bones of salmon or sole
butter
1 sprig of thyme
1/2 bay leaf
1 cup of white wine
1 1/2 quarts of water

PREPARATION OF FISH STOCK:

Wash the fish bones. Sweat bones in a stock pot with a little butter, 1 sprig of thyme, 1/2 bay leaf. Add 1 cup of white wine and 1 1/2 quarts of water. Boil slowly for 35 minutes, skim, strain. Do not salt.

INGREDIENTS FOR BECHAMEL:

2/3 ounces of flour
2/3 ounces of butter
1/2 pint of boiling milk

PREPARATION OF BECHAMEL:

Mix the flour with the butter. Cook very slowly for 15 minutes. Do not color. Let it cool. Add 1/2 pint of boiling milk. Let it boil very slowly for 15 minutes. Salt lightly.

INGREDIENTS FOR SAUCE:

1 1/2 pints of fish stock
1/2 pint of bechamel
1 pint of crème fraîche
1/2 pound of butter

PREPARATION OF SAUCE:

Strain 1 1/2 pints of fish stock into a saucepan. Add 1/2 pint of bechamel. Reduce for 10 minutes over high heat to obtain a creamy sauce. Add 1 pint of crème fraîche, bring to a boil. At once strain and add 1/2 pound of butter. Season if necessary.

SERVING:

Remove most of the skin. Mask the fish with the sauce. Serve the remaining sauce in a sauce boat.

J. Bowier,
L'Aubergade,
Pontchartrain, France

ESCALOPES OF SALMON WITH XERES VINEGAR

INGREDIENTS (per serving):

7 ounces of sliced salmon per
 person
1 small tomato
1 shallot
2 ounces of cream
2 ounces of butter
1 sauce spoon of Xeres vinegar
1 ounce of white wine
salt, pepper and chives

PREPARATION:

Poach the salmon with the shallot,
white wine, Xeres vinegar and
cream. Remove the salmon once it
is cooked. Then reduce the liquid
to 3/4 of its volume. Add the
chopped tomato, and the butter
at the end. Pour the sauce around
the salmon with some chives.

Michel Blanchet,
L'Ermitage,
Los Angeles, USA

ESCALOPE OF SALMON AND SALMON PUDDING WITH CHAMPAGNE SAUCE

Serves: 4

INGREDIENTS:

8 escalopes of salmon
 (about 2 ounces each)
3 ounces of sweet butter
a few leaves of chervil
salt and pepper

PREPARATION:

Slantingly cut thin slices from a boned fillet of salmon. (If necessary, place the slices between wax/or greaseproof paper, slightly moistening it so the salmon does not stick to it.) Using a heavy broad knife or a small wooden mallet, pound the escalopes to about 1/8 of an inch thick.
Arrange the salmon on four buttered plates and mask with the sauce (see right). Place the plates under high heat for one minute. Turn the warm pudding (see right) straight out of the moulds onto the middle of the plates, decorate with truffles, spoon a little more sauce around the pudding and sprinkle with chervil. Serve at once.

INGREDIENTS FOR
THE SALMON PUDDING:

4 ounces of salmon
1 egg
1 egg yolk
1/4 cup of cream
1/4 cup of milk
2 cups of slices of truffle for
 decoration

PREPARATION OF
THE SALMON PUDDING:

Dice the salmon. Mix egg, cream, milk, seasoning, and pour over the fish. Cool down the mixture and work it in the processor for one or two minutes and press it through a fine strainer.
Pour the mixture into small cups or moulds and poach in a double boiler in a preheated oven at 340° F for 20 to 25 minutes.

INGREDIENTS FOR THE
CHAMPAGNE SAUCE:

1 1/2 cups of fish stock
1 1/2 cups of champagne
1/2 cup of crème fraîche or
 heavy cream
salt and pepper

PREPARATION OF
THE CHAMPAGNE SAUCE:

Place the fish stock, the champagne and the cream in a saucepan and reduce it to 1/3 of its volume. Remove from the fire and beat in the remaining cold butter. Season with salt and pepper.

Willy Wyssenbach,
Continental,
Oslo, Norway

FRICASSEE OF SALMON

Serves: 4

INGREDIENTS:

5 ounces of salmon fillet,
 boned and skinned
2 ounces of butter
8 small carrots, the size of a little
 finger
8 spring onions
16 pieces of squash — a little
 smaller than the carrots
8 medium-sized leaves of spinach
1/2 tablespoon of fresh parsley
 greens
1/2 cup of white wine
1 1/2 cups of cream
1 tablespoon of beurre manié
salt and pepper

PREPARATION:

Clean and blanch the spring onions and carrots 3 to 5 minutes in separate waters, then chill in cold water with ice cubes. Cut the squash, blanch 2 minutes and chill in cold water, so that the vegetables keep their firmness and color.
Cut the salmon in small 1-inch cubes, season with salt and pepper. Heat 2/3 of the butter in a saute pan or low skillet, and just before it starts to color, add the salmon cubes which are turned around with a table fork in order to obtain a crust on all sides. Keep the skillet moderately warm all the time. With a lid or a large plate, cover nearly the whole skillet. Press down and pour out the frying butter. Replace the skillet on the stove, add the white wine and half of the cream. Let the salmon draw for 10 to 15 seconds close to the boiling point, then remove with a slotted spoon. Cover the fish and keep warm. Combine the stock with the remaining cream and reduce 1/3. Work in the beurre manié and strain the sauce into an oven-proof serving dish. Heat the blanched vegetables in the remaining butter, add the spinach, a few drops of water and a little salt. Place the fish and the vegetables in the sauce, sprinkle parsley on top and serve with small potatoes à l'anglaise.

Willy Wyssenbach,
Continental,
Oslo, Norway

ESTOUFFADE OF SALMON IN RED WINE SAUCE

(Estouffade de saumon au vin vieux)

Serves: 6

INGREDIENTS FOR THE SAUCE:

Head and bones from a 2 pound
 salmon
5 ounces of butter
1 bottle of red Bordeaux
1 1/2 quarts of water
4 white peppercorns
1 whole clove
1/2 cup of crème fraîche
8 ounces of glazed onions
10 ounces of champignons
5 ounces of sliced fresh pork fat
chervil

Mirepoix made from:
5 ounces of carrots
1 branch of celery
1 1/2 ounces of shallot

PREPARATION OF THE SAUCE:

Sweat the bones and head in
butter with the mirepoix. Add the
Bordeaux wine, the water, the
peppercorns and the clove.
Simmer for one and a half hours.
Remove the bones and the head,
process the rest in a blender, then
strain. Reduce the stock, after
adding the crème fraîche, to
desired consistency. Work in the
butter. Add the glazed onions, the
quartered browned champignons
and lightly browned sticks of the
pork.

INGREDIENTS:

2 pounds of fillets of salmon
6 eggs
1 ounce of vinegar
butter fried slices of bread, and
bread croutons

PREPARATION OF THE SALMON:

Dice the salmon into 1 inch
cubes, quickly brown them in a
non-stick frying pan (without fat).
Drain the salmon fat. Mix the
salmon cubes in the sauce, let
stew for 5 minutes. In the meantime, poach the eggs whole in the
vinegar and place them on the
bread slices. Place the salmon in
deep soup plates, pour over the
sauce. Garnish with the bread and
poached eggs. Decorate with
some croutons and sprinkle with
the chervil leaves.

*Lennart Engström,
Copenhague,
Paris, France*

SALMON IN CURRY SAUCE WITH WILD RICE

Serves: 4

INGREDIENTS:

1 pound 5 ounces of salmon fillet
 without skin, bones and fat
1 medium-sized green bell pepper
1 medium-sized red bell pepper
1 ounce of butter
2 teaspoons of curry powder
2 cups of heavy cream
1 tomato, scalded and seeded,
 diced
1 teaspoon of Mango Chutney
 (medium hot)
salt

PREPARATION:

Cut the salmon into 1 inch
squares. Blanch the bell peppers
in lightly salted water for 3 to 4
minutes, and cool in ice water or
running cold water. Remove the
skin if possible, and the seeds.
Dice the bell peppers or slice into
strips.
In a heavy skillet or a low-sided
saucepan, warm the butter, sweat
the lightly salted salmon pieces.
Sprinkle the curry powder and
add the heavy cream.
Bring the cream to a boil, cover,
reduce the heat and let the
salmon draw for 2 to 3 minutes.
Remove the salmon pieces with a
slotted spoon and keep warm and
covered so they do not dry out.
Reduce the sauce to desired
consistency, add the bell peppers,
the tomato and the chutney, and
if necessary some salt.
Arrange the salmon on a deep
serving dish or on plates with the
sauce on top.

INGREDIENTS FOR THE WILD RICE:

2 1/2 ounces of wild rice
4 ounces of long grain rice
3/4 ounce of butter
1/2 hard boiled egg

PREPARATION OF THE WILD RICE:

Rinse the wild rice several times
in a strainer and cook in lightly
salted water for 40 to 50 minutes
on a moderate heat. Drain and
dry the rice, mixing it with the
cooked white rice, the chopped
hard boiled egg and the butter.
Wild rice tastes better mixed with
ordinary rice.

*Willy Wyssenbach,
Continental,
Oslo, Norway*

FILLET OF SALMON WITH ASPARAGUS

Serves: 4

INGREDIENTS:

1 1/4 pounds of salmon fillet, skinned and boned
3 ounces of sweet butter
1 teaspoon of finely sliced chives
1 teaspoon of fresh parsley greens
1 cup of fish stock
1 cup of white wine
3/4 cup of cream
12 fresh asparagus
salt and pepper

PREPARATION:

Mix 2 ounces of the butter with the chives and the parsley. The remaining butter is brushed out in a roasting pan or an ovenproof dish.

Season the salmon, place it in the pan or dish, brush the butter mixture on it and pour enough of the fish stock and the white wine on the side of the fish so that it does not reach the butter. The remaining stock and wine is reduced to a glaze.

Put the pan in a preheated oven 350 to 400° F for 12 to 15 minutes, and after 5 minutes cover with an aluminum foil. Cook the asparagus and chill in cold water. The tops are set aside for decoration, the rest is sliced. The bottom part is pureed in a blender and strained through a cloth to remove the coarse fibers. Place the salmon on a serving dish, cover and keep warm. Work the remaining herb butter into the stock, reduce to the correct consistency and add the asparagus puree and the slices from the midpieces of the asparagus. Correct the seasoning – beat the cream until frothy and fold it into the sauce which is poured over the salmon. The warm asparagus tops are used for decorating.

Willy Wyssenbach,
Continental,
Oslo, Norway

HARBOR KETTLE

Serves: 4

INGREDIENTS:

1/2 of a fennel
  (preferably with the green top)
4 teaspoons of olive oil
8 fresh mussels
4 fresh scallops, cleaned and
  washed
8 scampi
2 cups of salmon stock
1 branch of kelp
12 salmon quenelles,
  1 ounce each
8 drops of Tabasco sauce
salt and pepper

PREPARATION:

Cut the fennel in long strips, keep
the green for the end. Quickly
blanch the fennel strips in boiling
water and cool in cold water. In a
saucepan, add the oil , the
mussels, the scallops, the scampi,
some salt, freshly ground pepper
and the fennel strips. Sweat for a
few seconds, add 1/2 cup of the
salmon stock and the kelp. Cover
and cook for 2 1/2 to 3 minutes.
Remove the shellfish, cover and
keep warm, but check that they
do not dry out. Remove the kelp
and bring the stock to a boil,
adding the quenelles. Remove the
pan from the fire, correct the
seasoning with possibly more salt,
pepper and Tabasco sauce. Distribute the shellfish and the salmon
quenelles evenly in hot deep soup
plates, and ladle the stock with
the fennel over the fish. Sprinkle
the green fennel on top, and
serve piping hot.

Willy Wyssenbach,
Continental,
Oslo, Norway

MOUSSE OF SALMON TOUT PARIS

(Mousse de saumon tout Paris)

Serves: 6

INGREDIENTS:

1 pound of skinless and boneless
 fresh salmon
salt, pepper, allspice
1/2 cup of fish velouté
2 egg whites
3 cups of heavy cream
fleurons
truffles

PREPARATION:

Process the salmon in a blender
with a little salt, pepper and allspice. Add the fish velouté and
the 2 egg whites and then process
again.
Add the heavy cream and mix for
a few seconds.
Pour it in a heavy buttered mould.
Poach for 6 to 7 minutes. Garnish
the sauce with fleurons and
truffles.
Serve it with lobster and
champagne.

Alain P. Sailhac,
Le Cirque,
New York, USA

POACHED ESCALOPE OF SALMON WITH LEEKS AND POTATOES, TRUFFLE BUTTER

(Escalope de saumon pochée aux poireaux et aux pommes de terre, beurre aux truffes)

Serves: 4

INGREDIENTS:

1 pound 5 ounces of fillet of
    salmon, cut into 8 slices
10 ounces of leeks, diced
7 ounces of raw potatoes, diced
5 ounces of butter
1/4 cup of vegetable bouillon
1 cup of fish stock
1/4 cup of truffle juice
1/4 cup of white port wine
3 shallots, chopped
1/4 cup of heavy cream
1 2/3 ounces of black truffles,
    chopped
1 tablespoon of leaves of chervil
salt, pepper, lemon juice and
    cayenne pepper

PREPARATION:

Lightly sauté the leeks and the potatoes in foaming butter, season with salt and pepper. Add the bouillon and reduce. Combine with a tablespoon of potato purée. Season. At the same time, combine and reduce to half the volume, the fish stock, the truffle juice, the port wine, and the shallots. Add the cream and reduce. Whip 3 1/3 ounces of butter, season and add the truffles.

Place the escalopes on a buttered baking dish, with a little fish stock, salt and pepper. Poach for 2 to 3 minutes in a hot oven, until pink in the center.
Place the leeks and the potatoes in the middle of the plate or the serving dish. Arrange the salmon on a mirror of sauce, and decorate with chervil leaves.

Hans Stucki,
Stucki Bruderholz,
Basel, Switzerland

POACHED SMOKED SALMON WITH EGG BUTTER AND CARROTS

Serves: 4

INGREDIENTS:

1 pound 4 ounces of smoked
  salmon
2 hard boiled eggs
4 ounces of sweet butter
1 pound of carrots

PREPARATION:

Cut the salmon into pieces of
about 2 1/2 ounces and place
these in unsalted boiling water
and let them draw for 8 to 10
minutes.
Melt the butter in a double boiler.
Cook the carrots and chop the
eggs coarsely.
Arrange the salmon on a dish. Mix
the chopped eggs in the butter
and serve it separately with the
carrots.
(A dish for the cold season.)

Willy Wyssenbach,
Continental,
Oslo, Norway

SALMON POACHED IN WHITE WINE WITH CUCUMBER AND WHITEFISH ROE

Serves: 4

This dish should be prepared just
before serving. The sauce is
quickly made, since the sour
cream is already thick and needs
only the flavor from the fish, the
wine and the cucumber.

INGREDIENTS:

4 slices of fresh salmon,
  5 3/4 ounces each
1 1/2 cups of dry white wine
2 tablespoons of white wine
  vinegar
1 quart of fish stock
2 cups of sour cream
1 1/2 cups of julienne from
  peeled cucumber
3 1/3 ounces of butter,
  at room temperature
1 1/2 ounces of salt
Cayenne pepper
3 1/3 ounces of whitefish roe

GARNISH:

mashed potatoes

PREPARATION:

Place the fish stock, the wine, the
vinegar and the salmon in a pan
and let simmer under cover for
about 8 minutes, depending on
thickness. Remove fish and place
on warm plates under aluminum
foil. Keep warm. Reduce the stock
down to a few tablespoons of
liquid.
Add the sour cream and the
cucumber julienne and cook for a
couple of minutes.

Remove the pan from the fire.
Work in the butter a dab at a time
and season with salt and a dash
of Cayenne. Heat the sauce, pour
it over the salmon steaks and top
with a spoonful of whitefish roe.
Serve at once with mashed
potatoes.

SALMON ROLLS WITH LUMPFISH MOUSSELINE AND SALMON ROE

Serves: 4

INGREDIENTS:

4 escalopes of salmon,
  4 ounces each
10 ounces of lumpfish fillet
3 1/3 ounces of champignons
6 tablespoons of breadcrumbs
6 egg whites
1 finely chopped onion
6 finely chopped morels
salt

INGREDIENTS FOR THE SAUCE:

1 cup of fish stock with
  4 teaspoons of Vermouth
1 cup of cream
1/2 pound of butter
8 crayfish with shells
2 ounces of salmon roe

GARNISH:

7 ounces of saffron rice

PREPARATION OF
THE LUMPFISH MOUSSELINE:

Process the lumpfish meat twice
in the blender until fine. Add
champignons and egg white. Put
aside in cool place or on ice. Stir
well, add the cream a little at a
time. Add the breadcrumbs,
season with salt.

PREPARATION OF THE SALMON ROLLS:

Place the escalopes on a table, sprinkle some milled salt, pipe the lumpfish mousseline along the middle of the salmon in two rows. Roll the escalopes together to form rolls.

Butter the bottom of a saucepan, sprinkle the finely chopped morels and the onion on top of the butter, and place the rolls in the pan. Add the fish stock and the vermouth and slowly steam under cover 4 to 5 minutes. Place the rolls on a plate or a dish and keep warm.

Reduce the fish stock and the cream to a creamy consistency, working in the cold butter. Bring to a boil.

Prepare the rice (cook) as indicated on the package, but add a little saffron.

Mask the bottom of a plate with the sauce, arrange the rice in the middle. Trim the sides of the rolls and place on the rice. Decorate with 2 crayfish with shelled tails and sprinkle some salmon roe on top.

Walter Nichtawitz,
Lasse's Catering,
Brevik, Norway

SALMON WITH CREAMY WHITEFISH SAUCE AND SMALL CUCUMBERS

To make a good sauce may take some time. This dish can be started the day before serving, since the sauce contains a fish stock that has to be greatly reduced.

Serves: 4

INGREDIENTS:

1 pound of fresh salmon, diced in even cubes
3 1/3 ounces of butter
2 tablespoons of whitefish roe
fresh chervil or parsley
1 cucumber (as thick as possible)

The cucumber is an important part of this dish. It is a finicky job, perhaps, but it can be done ahead of time; peel the cucumber, cut it in two lengthwise, remove the seeds and divide it into appropriately long strips. Fashion the cylinders with a potato peeler, reserving 1/2 cup of cucumber for the sauce. Cook in butter and its own juice. The juice will be used in the sauce. Serve the warm cucumbers as garnish with the salmon.

INGREDIENTS FOR THE FISH STOCK:

2 backbones and trimmings of flatfish
1 piece of cod or haddock (necks are fine, but without gills)
1 yellow onion, quartered
1 bay leaf
1 sprig of thyme
1 diced carrot
2 celery stalks
2 stems of parsley
water

PREPARATION FOR THE STOCK:

Place the bones and trimmings together with the vegetables and the spices in a saucepan with enough water to cover the fish. Bring slowly to a boil and let simmer for about 20 minutes. Skim well. Strain the stock through a cloth and let the liquid continue to cook on a slow fire until it has reduced to 1 cup.

INGREDIENTS FOR THE SAUCE:

1 cup of fish stock
1 cup of dry white wine
1 tablespoon of Noilly Prat (or similar vermouth)
2 shallots
1 2/3 ounces of champignons
1/2 cup of the remaining cucumber
1 1/2 cups of heavy cream
1 tablespoon of butter
2 tablespoons of whitefish roe

Order the fish and trimmings ahead of time. Clean and rinse the fish thoroughly in running cold water. Blood and gills may give a bitter taste to the stock.

PREPARATION FOR THE SAUCE:

Mix the wine, fish stock, the diced champignons, the remaining cucumber (without peel) and the finely chopped shallots. Cook until it is reduced to 1 cup. Strain the liquid from the solids and run these in a food processor. Strain and add to the liquid. Continue to cook, adding the cream, and reduce to the proper consistency.

Dilute sauce with the buttery liquid from the cucumbers, add the whitefish roe and process the sauce in the food processor until all the roe is crushed, giving the sauce its flavor. It is usually not necessary to season more, but nevertheless, check the seasoning. Just before serving, add a dab of butter.

PREPARATION OF THE SALMON:

Sweat the salmon in a hot frying pan with butter or in a dry non-stick pan. The salmon must be evenly cooked with a pink center. Place three to four spoons of the sauce on each warm plate. Place the salmon and the cucumbers on the sauce plus a little whitefish roe. Decorate with chervil or parsley.

Lennart Engström,
Copenhague,
Paris, France

SALMON SERVED AS IN THE LOIRE VALLEY

Serves: 4

INGREDIENTS:

1 fillet of salmon, boned, but with
  the skin on, weighing between 1
  pound 8 ounces and 1 pound 11
  ounces
2 2/3 ounces of finely chopped
  shallots
1 1/3 ounces of butter
2 cups of white wine
  (Pouilly-Fumé)
1 cup of fish stock
1 cup of crème fraîche
3 1/3 ounces of sweet, ripe
  grapes, peeled, seeded and
  sliced in two
salt and pepper

PREPARATION:

Butter a long pan, spread the
shallots on the bottom, moisten
with some white wine and let the
shallots steam a few minutes.
Season the salmon with salt and
pepper, place it in the pan with
the skin up, add the remaining
wine and the fish stock and set
the pan covered with aluminum
foil in a preheated oven at 320° F
for about 12 to 15 minutes.

Arrange the salmon on a dish,
remove the skin, cover the dish
with foil or a lid while the
poaching liquid is being reduced
to glaze. Add the cream and strain
the sauce which is poured around
the fish. The grapes, already
prepared, are quickly turned over
in a frying pan with butter and
arranged on the fish.

Willy Wyssenbach,
Continental,
Oslo, Norway

SALMON BRAIDS WITH LIME AND CHERVIL SAUCE

Serves: 4

INGREDIENTS FOR
THE SALMON:

8 slices of salmon, cut lengthwise
salt and pepper

INGREDIENTS FOR THE SAUCE:

1 cup of fish stock
1/2 cup of champagne
2 2/3 ounces of butter
1 shallot, finely chopped
1 to 3 tablespoons of whipped
  cream
1 lime
1 tablespoon of chervil
salt and pepper

GARNISH:

1 pound 5 ounces of small
  zucchini
1 bunch of chervil
oil
butter
salt and pepper
rice

PREPARATION OF THE SAUCE:

Cook the fish stock, the champagne and the shallot. Reduce to 1/4 of the volume. Work in the ice cold butter and strain. Then carefully add the shredded lime rind.
Mix in the lime juice, the whipped cream and some leaves of chervil. Process in the blender until foamy, and season with salt and pepper.

PREPARATION OF THE SALMON:

Season the salmon lightly with salt and pepper. Place the fish in aluminum foil or a buttered paper on a non-stick pan, and steam the salmon for about 3 minutes. It should not be cooked through.

PREPARATION OF THE GARNISH:

Wash the zucchini and slice paper-thin. Sauté quickly (1 minute) in a hot frying pan with some oil and butter. Season lightly with salt and pepper and mix with the chopped chervil, and taste.

SERVING:

Place the fillet on a hot plate, covered with zucchini. Twist the other fillet to make it look like a braid and place it on top of the zucchini.
Mask with hot sauce, and sprinkle with chervil.
The remaining zucchini and the rice are served on the side.

Gutbert Fallert,
Talmühle,
Sasbachwalden, West Germany

SALMON SOUFFLÉ WITH PIKE MOUSSELINE

(Saumon "Maître Schlegel")

Serves: 4

This dish was one of the specialties of the Palace Hotel in Lucerne. The dish was invented in honor of Otto Schlegel who was head chef in this hotel for 26 years. Otto Schlegel also spent 26 seasons in the world-famous Palace Hotel, Gstaad. I had the pleasure of working for four very enjoyable and instructive seasons with Mr. Schlegel, a superb master of his profession.

INGREDIENTS:

18 ounces of salmon fillet
salt, freshly ground pepper
1 teaspoon of finely chopped
  shallot
5 ounces of mousseline of pike
4 scampi without their shells
3/4 ounce of butter
4 fluid ounces of white wine
4 fluid ounces of fish stock
2 fluid ounces of Noilly Prat
3/4 pint of heavy cream
2 ounces of butter, to finish
a little sorrel, cut into strips
2 fluid ounces of lobster sauce

METHOD:

Skin and bone the fillet, cutting it into 4 portions.
Cover the seasoned salmon portions evenly with the pike mousseline.
Lay the the seasoned scampi on top, pressing them gently into the mousseline.
Grease a sautoir and sprinkle with the finely chopped shallot.
Arrange the salmon portions in it. Add the white wine and fish stock, cover and poach in the oven. Remove the fish and keep hot.
To the stock, add the Noilly Prat and reduce. Add the cream and reduce until the required consistency is achieved.
Gradually work in the butter, add sorrel and season with salt and pepper.
Place the salmon briefly under the grill or in a hot oven to give a good color.
Place the sauce in a suitable dish and arrange the salmon on it.
Carefully cover the scampi with the well seasoned lobster sauce.

MOUSSELINE OF PIKE:

(Mousseline de brochet)

Serves: 4

INGREDIENTS FOR THE MOUSSELINE OF PIKE:

9 ounces of pike flesh,
  without skin and bones
salt
freshly ground pepper
a little cayenne and nutmeg
1/2 pint of heavy cream

METHOD FOR THE MOUSSELINE OF PIKE:

Mince the pike flesh finely and place in a bowl on ice.
Season with salt, pepper, nutmeg and cayenne.
Work in the heavy cream, using a wooden spoon.
Rub the mixture through a fine sieve and keep cool.
Season again and store in a cool place.
Note! It is very important that the heavy cream be worked in slowly and thoroughly so that the cream and pike flesh bind together. This mousseline may be used for quenelles and also as stuffing for such dishes as tronçons de turbot.

FISH STOCK:

(Fond de poisson)

Makes one quart of fish stock

INGREDIENTS FOR THE FISH STOCK:

2 pounds of broken up fish bones
  and trimmings
2 ounces of white mirepoix
  (onions,. white of leek, celeriac,
  fennel leaves, dill)
1 1/4 ounces of mushroom
  trimmings
3/4 ounces of butter
6 fluid ounces of white wine
2 pints of water
salt, freshly ground pepper

METHOD FOR THE FISH STOCK:

Thoroughly wash the fish bones and trimmings.
Sweat the mirepoix and the mushroom trimmings in the butter.
Add the fish bones and trimmings, white wine and water. Simmer for 20 minutes, occasionally skimming and removing the fat.
Strain through a cloth or fine sieve and season with salt and pepper.

Note! In order to produce a good fish stock, only the bones of fresh white fish (sole, turbot) should be used.

LOBSTER SAUCE:

(Sauce homard)

Serves: 4

INGREDIENTS FOR THE LOBSTER SAUCE:

1 lobster (9 to 10 ounces)
2 fluid ounces of olive oil
2 ounces of mirepoix
2 ounces of diced tomatoes
2 fluid ounces of Cognac
4 fluid ounces of white wine
18 fluid ounces of fish stock
a little fresh dill and tarragon
a little meat glaze
2 ounces of butter
salt, freshly ground pepper

METHOD FOR THE LOBSTER SAUCE:

Place the lobster in boiling water for one minute to kill it. Cut the body in half and chop it into pieces, remove stomach and save the coral.

Heat the olive oil in a sautoir, add the lobster pieces and, using a wooden spatula, sauté on all sides (until the shell is completely red). Add the mirepoix and tomatoes and sweat well.

Flame with the brandy and then add the white wine.

Add the fish stock and chopped herbs and bring to a boil.

Take the lobster pieces and remove the meat from the shell.

Cut the lobster shell as finely as possible and return to the stock.

Simmer for approximately 30 minutes on a low heat.

Add the meat glaze and reduce the stock to one third its original volume.

Add the lobster coral, mixed with the butter, to bind it.

Strain the sauce and season to taste.

Note! The lobster meat may be used for various other dishes, for instance, in a cold buffet.

MEAT GLAZE:

(Glace de viande)

Reduce 16 pints of brown veal stock or clear brown stock to 1 3/4 pints in a suitable saucepan on low heat. During the reduction keep transferring the liquid into smaller saucepans. It is important that the edge of the saucepan be kept clean by means of a spatula.

Anton Mosimann,
The Dorchester,
London, England

SALMON WITH CAVIAR AND OAT FLAKE BLINIS

(Saumon au caviar et blinis aux flocons d'avoine)

Serves: 6

INGREDIENTS:

12 pieces of salmon,
  each about 3 ounces
2 cups of fish stock
2 shallots
2 cups of Riesling d'Alsace
salt and pepper
cream
2 ounces of caviar

DECORATION:

One zucchini, one carrot, julienne
of red bell peppers.

BLINIS WITH OAT FLAKES:

3 ounces of oat flakes
2 whole eggs
1 cup of milk
salt, pepper and nutmeg
butter

Mix the above ingredients an hour
before to let the oat flakes swell.
Then fry the blinis.

PREPARATION OF THE SALMON:

Poach the salmon with the
chopped shallots, the Riesling and
the fish stock.
Remove the salmon and reduce
the stock. Add the cream and
reduce once more until the right
consistency. Season according to
taste.
Place the salmon on a dish.
Decorate with the zucchini, the
fluted carrot and the red bell
pepper julienne. Garnish with the
caviar and the blinis.

Émile Jung,
Au Crocodile,
Strasbourg, France

SALMON SUPREME WITH BLACK NOODLES

(Suprême de saumon aux nouilles noires)

Serves: 4

The very unusual black noodles in this recipe – made with squid ink – accompany the salmon perfectly.

INGREDIENTS:

4 fillets of salmon, about 5 ounces each, boned and skinned
4 sprigs of basil
3 ounces of filo paste, about 4 sheets (see separate recipe)
3/4 ounce of shallots, finely chopped
2 teaspoons of garlic, finely chopped
7 ounces of ripe tomatoes, skinned, seeded and diced
1 tablespoon of cut chives
1 quantity of black noodles (see separate recipe)
salt and finely ground pepper

PREPARATION:

Season the salmon fillets with salt and pepper, and place a sprig of basil on top of each. Dip each sheet of filo paste momentarily in boiling water, and then in cold water. Remove immediately. Wrap each salmon fillet in a blanched filo sheet. Steam fillets for 3 to 4 minutes. Sauté the shallots and garlic in a non-stick pan, stirring constantly, until transparent. Add the tomatoes and sauté for about 1 minute. Add the cut chives and season with salt and pepper. Cook the black noodles in boiling salted water for about 3 minutes, until *al dente*. Drain the noodles, reserving 2 tablespoons of the cooking water, and rinse quickly in cold water. Toss the noodles with the reserved water in a saucepan over gentle heat, then season with salt and pepper. Put the noodles on four individual plates and arrange the salmon on top. Make a small cut in the top of the pastry and gently ease out one of the basil leaves from the sprig. Garnish with well-seasoned tomatoes.

FILO PASTE:

This pastry – the only one used in Cuisine Naturelle – is here made without oil or butter. It must be rolled extremely thin, and when baked, is crisp and light.

Makes 1 1/4 to 1 1/2 pounds

11 ounces of strong white bread flour
4 ounces of wheat flour
1/2 teaspoon of salt
1/2 pint of water

PREPARATION OF THE FILO PASTE:

Sift the flour, the wheat flour and salt together into a bowl. Make a well in the center.
Put about half the water into the well, and gradually draw the flour into the water, mixing smoothly and evenly. Add the remaining water and mix until the dough is smooth and does not stick to the hands. Cover the dough with a damp cloth and leave to rest for 1 to 2 hours in a cool place. This allows it to develop its elasticity fully. Cut the dough into quarters, and cover the pieces not being rolled with a damp cloth. Start rolling one piece out, gradually making the sheet thinner and thinner. Use plenty of flour, and it helps to warm the dough to make it pliable – cover with an inverted hot aluminum bowl.
If the dough sheet becomes too large and unwieldy, cut in half and continue to roll. When rolled as thin as possible, place the sheet over the back of the hand, and pull gently down from the edges to stretch even more. Work carefully so that it does not break. Roll the other pieces of dough in the same way, and cover dough and sheets at all times with a damp cloth. Use sheets as quickly as possible.

HOME-MADE EGG NOODLES WITH INK:

(Nouilles à l'encre)

7 ounces of strong plain flour, sifted
1 ounce of semolina
1 egg
a pinch of salt
8 teaspoons of reduced squid ink, if necessary add a little warm water

PREPARATION OF THE EGG NOODLES:

Buy very fresh squid with unbroken ink sacs, so that as much ink as possible can be collected. About 2 1/4 pounds squid should provide enough ink to reduce, by simmering, to the required quantity of 8 teaspoons. If necessary, make the amount up with a little warm water. Add ink, or ink and water, to the flour mixture instead of the hot water in the recipe for Home-Made Egg Noodles, along with the eggs.

Anton Mosimann,
The Dorchester,
London, England

SMOKED SALMON WITH WHITEFISH ROE AND EGG

Serves: 1

INGREDIENTS:

1 slice of smoked salmon,
  1 2/3 ounces
2 quail's eggs
2 teaspoons of salmon roe
1 teaspoon of whitefish roe
1/4 cup of heavy cream
1/4 cup of good fish stock
1 ounce of chanterelles
some chopped shallot
1 tablespoon of vinegar
1 sprig of dill or chervil,
  for decoration

PREPARATION:

Thoroughly clean the chanterelles and sauté in a little butter together with the shallot.
Cook the stock and the cream for 2 minutes. The sauce must be smooth but not thick. Season with salt and pepper.
In a saucepan put 1 quart of water and 1 tablespoon of vinegar. Bring to a boil. Break the eggs into the liquid. Reduce the heat so the water simmers. Poach for 2 minutes. Remove the eggs with a slotted spoon and trim.

SERVING:

Arrange the salmon on a plate. Pour the sauce around the fish. Distribute the chanterelles on the sauce, but make 4 small holes for the eggs and the caviar.
Set the plate in a warm oven for 20 seconds.
Decorate the plate with a sprig of dill or chervil and serve at once.

Jean-Louis Lieffroy,
Falsled Kro,
Millinge, Fyn, Denmark

RAGOUT OF SALMON IN FLAKY PASTRY HOUSE

Serves: 4

INGREDIENTS:

1 pound 4 ounces of salmon,
  tail part
1/2 of an onion
1 teaspoon of butter
1/2 cup of white wine
1/2 cup of fish stock
salt
1/2 cup of heavy cream
2 sheets of flaky pastry
8 asparagus points

PREPARATION:

Chop the onion finely and sweat it without it taking color. Add the white wine and the fish stock. Cook for 5 minutes.
Dice the salmon, which has been boned and skinned, into large cubes. Poach the salmon cubes for 3 minutes and season with salt. Add the cream and reduce.
Divide the flaky pastry sheets into 4 equal parts and bake them in a preheated oven of 390° F for about 20 minutes, until golden brown. Again divide the pastry pieces in two.
Distribute the salmon cubes and the asparagus points on 4 pieces of flaky pastry. Spoon the cream sauce on top, and place the remaining pastry pieces on top as lids.
Serve at once.

Walter Nichtawitz,
Lasse's Catering,
Brevik, Norway

TURBAN OF SALMON, AURORA SAUCE

(Turban de saumon, sauce aurore)

Serves: 6

INGREDIENTS:

3 pounds of fresh salmon
2 egg whites
2 cups of crème fraîche
salt, pepper and nutmeg
8 to 10 good-sized crayfish
1 onion
2 carrots
1 leek
white wine
Cognac
thyme, bay leaf
1 2/3 ounces of butter
1 tablespoon of tomato paste
chives, tarragon and chervil

PREPARATION:

Cut the salmon into thin escalopes. Butter and oil a savarin mould, 7 inches in diameter. Line the mould with the escalopes. Pound the remaining salmon and work in the egg whites. Rub through a fine sieve. Place in a terrine and put this on ice.
Continue to work it with one cup of crème fraîche, a little at a time. Season with salt, pepper and nutmeg. Add a spoonful of chopped tarragon, chervil and chive. Fill the mould with the mixture and place a wax-paper on top. Poach in a bain-marie for 20 to 25 minutes. When the mixture is cooked, let rest for a few minutes. Turn it around on a rack to drain the liquid which is inside the mould.

Gut the crayfish (remove the intestines), cook them à la Bordelaise, shell them, reserving 6 bodies for decorating the dish. Pound the rest and make a sauce as à l'Américaine. Strain and add the cream and work in the butter. Season and turn out the mould on a round dish. Add the julienne of carrot and leek, steamed in butter. Dispose the shelled crayfish in the center and mask with the sauce. Decorate with the crayfish bodies around the turban and sprinkle with chopped tarragon.

Jacques Corbonnois,
Leves, France

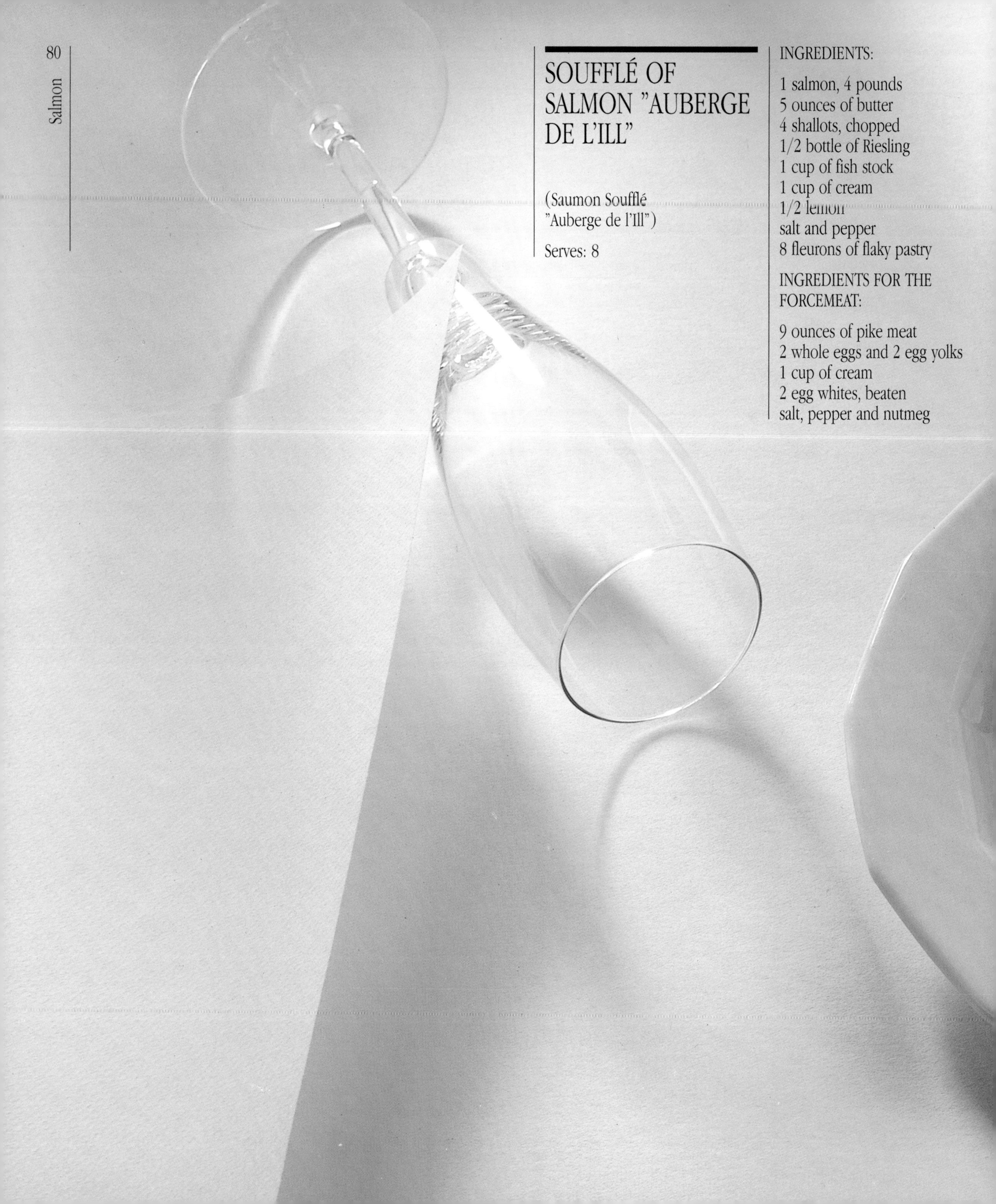

SOUFFLÉ OF SALMON "AUBERGE DE L'ILL"

(Saumon Soufflé "Auberge de l'Ill")

Serves: 8

INGREDIENTS:

1 salmon, 4 pounds
5 ounces of butter
4 shallots, chopped
1/2 bottle of Riesling
1 cup of fish stock
1 cup of cream
1/2 lemon
salt and pepper
8 fleurons of flaky pastry

INGREDIENTS FOR THE FORCEMEAT:

9 ounces of pike meat
2 whole eggs and 2 egg yolks
1 cup of cream
2 egg whites, beaten
salt, pepper and nutmeg

PREPARATION:

Fillet the salmon or have the fishmonger do it for you. Cut the fillet into 8 pieces.
For the forcemeat: finely grind the pike meat, put in the blender with the eggs (2 whole and 2 yolks), salt, pepper and a small pinch of nutmeg. Process and slowly add the cream.

Put the forcemeat in a bowl and refrigerate. Beat the egg whites and fold in carefully with the well-chilled forcemeat.
Cover each piece with the forcemeat in the form of a dome. Place each piece on a buttered plate, add a little salt and the chopped shallots. Moisten with the Riesling and the fish stock and place in the oven. Let simmer for 15 to 20 minutes. Remove the salmon and place on a serving dish. Keep warm.

Pour the remaining liquid in a sautoir, add the cream and reduce. Work in the well-chilled butter in small portions. Add the lemon juice. If necessary, season and pour the sauce *around* the salmon. Decorate with the pastry fleurons.

Marc Haeberlin,
Auberge de l'Ill,
Ribeauvillé, France

STEAMED SALMON IN SOYA SAUCE

Serves: 4

INGREDIENTS:

4 pieces of salmon from a boned
  fillet, about 6 ounces each
3 ounces of fresh bean sprouts
1/4 cup of meat stock
1 cup of soya sauce
1 ounce of fresh butter
3/4 ounce of fresh, grated ginger
4 sprigs of fresh dill for
  decoration
salt and a little freshly ground
  pepper

PREPARATION:

Pour some water in a fish kettle
or other kettle that has a rack on
the bottom. The water must not
reach the rack.
Rub the meaty side of the salmon
with salt and a little pepper. Place
the salmon pieces on the rack and
steam under cover for about 8 to
10 minutes.

Steam the bean sprouts in the
meat stock for a few minutes,
drain but keep the stock and set
aside the bean sprouts and keep
warm. Reduce the stock to glaze
and add the soya sauce, heat
without allowing it to boil, and
with a whisk beat the butter into
the sauce. Add the grated ginger.
Remove the skin from the salmon,
arrange the fillets on a dish or a
plate, sprinkle the bean sprouts
on top and decorate with the dill.
Spoon the sauce around the fish.

Willy Wyssenbach,
Continental,
Oslo, Norway

WARM FROGS' LEGS SALAD AND FINGER SIZED SALMON FILLETS WITH CHIVES

(Cuisses de grenouilles en salade tiède et goujonnettes de saumon sauvage à la ciboulette)

Serves: 4

INGREDIENTS:

30 pieces of frog or about 2 pounds
1 pound 4 ounces of boned fillet of salmon
7 ounces of butter
sprigs of chervil and dill

INGREDIENTS FOR THE SAUCE AIGRELETTE:

1/2 pint of mayonnaise sauce (1/4 olive oil and 3/4 peanut oil)
1/2 glass of fish stock with white wine and spices or light fish stock, well seasoned
1 teaspoon of wine or xeres vinegar.
juice of one lemon
2 tablespoons of chives, snipped
1/2 tablespoon of chopped tarragon
salt and freshly ground pepper

PREPARATION:

Cook the frogs about 8 minutes in butter without coloring them, in one or two large pans on a moderate heat. Season well with salt and the freshly ground pepper. At the end of the cooking, let the frogs become tepid before boning the legs so they keep their original shape. Put aside in a saucepan, reserving some of the liquid.

Prepare the sauce aigrelette. It should not resemble a mayonnaise. Its consistency should be lighter and more fluid. Add the ingredients gradually until the sauce reaches a consistency that lightly films the spoon. Add the herbs and season.

With a sharp knife cut pieces the size of a finger from the fillet of salmon. Place in a fire-proof dish, lightly buttered. Put aside and heat the oven to its maximum.

At the time of serving, pour part of the sauce aigrelette over the frogs' legs, season and place on low heat while stirring with a wooden spatula.

In the meantime, sprinkle the pieces of salmon with a little water and place in the oven. The cooking will take only 2 to 3 minutes.

SERVING:

Using soup plates, arrange the tepid frogs' legs salad, dome shaped, in the middle and spoon the remaining sauce aigrelette around the frogs on the plates. Arrange the salmon pieces on top of the sauce around the frogs (about 2 to 3 per plate). Decorate with the sprigs of chervil and dill. Serve at once.

Georges Blanc,
Vonnas, France

SALMON ROLLS IMPERIAL

Serves: 10

INGREDIENTS FOR
THE SALMON:

3 pounds of salmon fillet
1 pound 4 ounces of turbot fillet
30 oysters (Imperial)
1 cup of heavy cream
blanched leaves of spinach
salt, pepper
Noilly Prat
dry white wine

PREPARATION OF THE SALMON:

Run the turbot in a food processor, then through a fine sieve. Place a bowl with the turbot on ice and keep in a cool place 20 minutes. Season the turbot with salt and freshly ground pepper. Slowly fold in the heavy cream. Season with Noilly Prat. Open the oysters, reserving the juice for the sauce. Enrobe 20 of the oysters in spinach leaves. Slice the salmon in 10 escalopes and flatten them. Lightly salt the escalopes and cover them with turbot forcemeat. Place 2 oysters on each escalope and roll up the escalope. Place the salmon rolls in a buttered skillet, adding the juice from the oysters and dry white wine. Poach for 10 minutes on slow heat.

INGREDIENTS FOR THE SAUCE:

3 cups of stock from the salmon
  rolls and fish stock
2 cups of heavy cream
3 ounces of butter
10 oysters, trimmed

PREPARATION OF THE SAUCE:

Reduce the stock and the heavy cream until desired consistency. Dice the remaining oysters and, with the cold butter, work them into the sauce.

Peter G. Hinz,
Haerlin,
Hamburg, West Germany

TWIN FILLETS OF SALMON

(Filets de saumon aux deux cuissons)

Serves: 6

Carefully and delicately clean a small salmon. After drying, take one fillet and leave the bone on the second fillet.

INGREDIENTS FOR THE FIRST FILLET:

1 fresh salmon,
 about 5 pounds
1 pound of green asparagus
2 bunches of chervil
5 ounces of butter

PREPARATION OF THE FIRST FILLET:

After skinning the fillet, cut 6 nice slices from that first fillet. Set aside with the trimmings in a cool place.
Clean the asparagus and cook the spears in water. Cool and set aside. Wash, dry and finely chop the chervil leaves and sauté a few seconds in browned butter and then mix them with the rest of the butter to a paste. Pass through a fine sieve and set aside to cool.

INGREDIENTS:

1 2/3 ounces of butter

PREPARATION:

A few minutes ahead, season the salmon slices, then sauté them in clarified butter on a brisk fire, being careful to keep them soft. Set aside and keep warm with the asparagus.

INGREDIENTS FOR THE SABAYON:

1 cup of champagne
1 1/2 cups of heavy cream
2 tablespoons Hollandaise sauce

PREPARATION OF THE SABAYON:

Remove excessive fat from the skillet and deglaze with champagne without reducing too much. Add cream, reduce and add a few tablespoons of Hollandaise sauce. Add this to the chervil butter, season and top off with a dash of champagne.

INGREDIENTS FOR THE SECOND FILLET:

3 1/3 ounces of shallots
10 ounces of tomatoes
4 cloves of garlic
thyme, bay leaf
1 bottle of red Hermitage wine

PREPARATION OF THE SECOND FILLET:

Prepare a fish stock with the head and some trimmings of the salmon and some red wine. On a bed of shallot, tomato, garlic, thyme and bay leaf, place the second fillet, with the bone downwards. Moisten to half the height of the fish with red wine and stock. Bring to simmer and let cook on a slow heat, basting often. When ready set aside and keep warm.

INGREDIENTS FOR THE CRAYFISH:

18 crayfish
1/2 cup of dry white wine
1 2/3 ounces of onion
1 2/3 ounces of carrot
1 bouquet garni

PREPARATION OF THE CRAYFISH:

Gut the crayfish. Bring court bouillon to the boil, add crayfish, and cook for one minute. Drain and shell the tails and set aside. Crush the bodies and make a crayfish butter. When ready, strain and set aside in the refrigerator to harden.

INGREDIENTS:

3/4 ounce of heavy cream

PREPARATION:

Reduce the braising stock after it has been strained. Add a little cream and work in the crayfish butter. Check the seasoning, set aside and keep warm.
Lift the fillet from its backbone and cut into six parts. Keep warm.

GARNISHES:

1) Mousseline of salmon with ragoût of frogs' legs:

2 eggs
1 cup of crème fleurette
13 ounces of frogs' legs
1 ounce of butter
1 ounce of shallots
1 bunch of chives
1 bunch of watercress
1/2 cup of champagne
1/2 cup of heavy cream

With the rest of the first fillet (about 7 ounces) and two eggs and whipped cream, make a light mousseline.
Season the frogs' legs and rapidly sauté them in butter. Add the finely diced shallot, some chives and coarsely chopped watercress. Deglaze with champagne, cover, reduce to half the volume, add some cream and let cook for a few minutes.
Remove the meat from the legs and set aside with the reduced and seasoned sauce.
Line six buttered half spheric moulds with the mousseline of salmon. Place one tablespoon of the ragoût of frogs' legs in each mould and fill up with the mousseline. Slowly poach in a bain-marie. After resting, unmould, mask with some sauce and garnish.

GARNISHES:

2) Soft carp roes with tomato and basilicum in flaky pastry:

7 ounces of soft carp roes or other fish roe
10 ounces of flaky pastry
1 egg

Clean the soft roes and lightly poach in a court bouillon. Using a six-turn flaky pastry dough, cut out six small fish-shaped pieces. After brushing them with egg yolk, bake in oven and then take off the tops, carving out the insides. Reserve the tops.

1 pound of tomatoes
2 cloves of garlic
1 bouquet garni
3 1/3 ounces of butter
1 bunch of basilicum
1 2/3 ounces of flour
1 2/3 ounces of butter
1 lemon

Chop the tomatoes coarsely and add some garlic. After cooking, pass through a sieve, add some butter and a little chopped basilicum. Set aside.
Cut slices from the roe, season with salt and pepper, dip in flour and sauté in hot butter. When ready sprinkle with lemon juice and place them in the pastry boats. Mask with the tomato sauce. Place the tops on the pastry, brush with butter.

SERVING ON THE PLATE:

While all the preparations are being kept warm, mask one side of each plate with the sabayon au champagne, and the other with the sauce à l'Hermitage. Place the fillets on their respective sauces. Arrange the asparagus spears around the sautéed fillet, and the crayfish tails around the braised fillet.
Place the mousseline on the champagne sauce and the pastry fishes on the Hermitage sauce.
Serve very hot.

Jean-Luc Danjou,
Massy, France

BAKED SALMON WITH SOUR CREAM STUFFING

Serves: 6

INGREDIENTS:

4 to 6 pounds of dressed salmon
1 1/2 teaspoons of salt
sour cream stuffing (see below)
2 tablespoons of melted fat or oil
small skewers or toothpicks

PREPARATION:

Clean, wash and dry the fish. Sprinkle inside and out with salt. Stuff fish loosely. Close opening with small skewers or toothpicks. Place fish in a well-greased baking pan. Brush with fat. Bake in a moderate oven, 350° F, for approximately 1 hour or until fish flakes easily when tested with a fork. Baste occasionally with fat. Remove skewers.

INGREDIENTS FOR
SOUR CREAM STUFFING:

3/4 cup of chopped celery
1/2 cup of chopped onion
1/4 cup of melted fat or oil
1 quart of dry bread crumbs
1 teaspoon of salt
1/2 cup of sour cream
1/4 cup of diced peeled lemon
2 tablespoons of grated lemon rind
1 teaspoon of paprika

PREPARATION:

Cook celery and onion in fat until tender. Combine all ingredients and mix thoroughly. Makes approximately 1 quart of stuffing.

ESCALOPES OF SALMON WITH NETTLES

Serves: 1

INGREDIENTS:

1/2 cup of good fish stock made from bones and trimmings of sole
1/2 cup of dry white wine
3/4 ounce of sweet butter
1/4 cup of crème fraîche
a small pinch of ground fennel and anise, salt and freshly ground white pepper (from mill)
1/2 ounce of young, quickly blanched, coarsely chopped nettles (one should use the first nettles that come up in spring, about 1/2 inch long)
4 ounces of fresh salmon cut in 2 thin escalopes, about 2 ounces each (cut from a 15 – 18 pound salmon)
2 young small carrots with a little green

PREPARATION:

Reduce by half the fish stock and the white wine and work in the butter with a whisk. Add the crème fraîche that has been seasoned with the anise, fennel, salt and white pepper. Put in the nettles.
Brush butter on a large plate and place the escalopes of salmon, add a little salt and place on a rack in the preheated oven at 480 degrees F. for 2 – 3 minutes. Heat the carrots in lightly salted water.
Mask the escalopes of salmon with the nettle sauce and garnish with the carrots or other seasonal vegetables and fleurons.

Manfred Mahnkopf,
Grand Hôtel,
Stockholm, Sweden

SALMON IN FLAKY PASTRY WITH MINT SAUCE

Serves: 4

INGREDIENTS FOR THE SALMON:

1 pound 5 ounces of salmon fillet
10 ounces of flaky pastry
salt

INGREDIENTS FOR THE SALMON FORCEMEAT:

7 ounces of salmon fillet
1 teaspoon of Pernod
1 cup of cream
salt
2 tablespoons of whipped cream

INGREDIENTS FOR THE SAUCE:

1 cup of fish stock
1/2 cup of white wine
2 tablespoons of crème fraîche
3 tablespoons of whipped cream
2 sprigs of mint
2 2/3 ounces of butter
salt
lemon juice

PREPARATION OF THE FORCEMEAT:

Make a smooth forcemeat with the salmon, the cream, the salt and the Pernod in the processor. Rub the mixture through a fine sieve and fold in the whipped cream, on ice.

PREPARATION OF THE SALMON:

Season the fillet, spread the forcemeat on top and wrap it all in the flaky pastry sheet. Bake it in a preheated oven at 390° F to 430° F, until golden brown.

PREPARATION OF THE MINT SAUCE:

Pour the fish stock and the white wine in a pan and reduce to a syrupy consistency. Work the mint in a processor to a fine purée and add it to the reduction together with the crème fraîche and the whipped cream. Work in the cold butter. Season with salt and the lemon juice.

SERVING:

Cut the salmon in slices and arrange on plates. Mask with the sauce, without wetting the pastry.

Wolf-Dieter Klunker,
Fischereihafenrestaurant,
Hamburg, West Germany

ESCALOPES OF SALMON WITH CABBAGE LEAVES BAKED IN PAPILLOTTE

(Escalope de saumon en papillotte au choux frisé)

Serves: 6

INGREDIENTS:

6 escalopes of salmon,
  5 ounces each
1 head of cabbage
6 tomatoes
3 1/2 ounces of shallots
7 ounces of butter
1 bunch of chives
2 ounces of parsley
1 lemon
6 sheets of wax-paper
1/2 cup of fish stock
1/4 cup of dry sherry
salt and pepper

PREPARATION:

Blanch the cabbage leaves in plenty of water, chill and trim the stalks. Peel the tomatoes, remove seeds, and dice. Chop the shallots and steam in 2 ounces of butter. Chop the parsley and the chives. Peel the outer layer of the lemon, leaving the white part, and cut in 12 slices. Fold the sheets of wax-paper in two and butter the insides. On the lower inside part of the paper, place two leaves of cabbage taken from the heart and place the diced tomatoes as well

as the steamed shallots, season with salt and pepper. Place an escalope of salmon on this bed, sprinkle with the chives and parsley and place two slices of lemon on top, season with salt and pepper, add a dab of butter and moisten with a little sherry and fish stock.
Close the papillottes, folding the edges over all around the envelopes. Place in a preheated oven (530 degrees F.) for 3 to 4 minutes.

SERVING:

Dress on a warm plate, serve at once, open the papillotte with a knife and fork in front of the guest.

1. ACCOMPANIED BY THESE THREE PURÉES:

1 generous pound of celery root
1 generous pound of carrots
1 generous pound of beans
3 1/2 ounces of butter
1/2 cup of cream
salt, pepper and nutmeg
2 onions

Clean and peel the vegetables. Boil the celery root à l'Anglaise, steam the carrots in butter with an onion and blanch the beans. Steam the second chopped onion. Make a smooth purée of each of the vegetables:
celery root:
add a dab of butter and 1/4 cup of cream, salt, pepper and nutmeg.
carrots:
add 1/4 cup of cream, salt and pepper.
beans:
add the steamed onion, salt and pepper.

Serving:

Dress the three purées in domes on a dessert plate.

2. ACCOMPANIED BY STEAMED WHEAT SEMOLINA:

5 ounces of wheat semolina
1/4 cup of olive oil
3 1/2 ounces of peas,
  deep-frozen,
or 1 pound of fresh
3 1/2 ounces of red pimento
1 teaspoon of fenugreek,
salt and pepper.

Moisten the semolina with 2 tablespoons of olive oil and 1/4 cup of water, mix and work the mixture well, adding fenugreek, salt and pepper. Set aside for 3 hours. In the meantime steam the red pimento julienne in olive oil. Steam the semolina in a couscousiere for 30 minutes, add the peas and steam for another 30 minutes.

Carlos Grootaert,
Auberge du Pré Bossu,
Moudeyres, France

MOUSSELINE OF SALMON IN FLAKY PASTRY QUEEN SILVIA

(La mousseline de saumon en feuilletage Reine Silvia)

A lightly truffled stuffing made with fresh salmon on a bed of spinach, baked in flaky pastry.

Serves: 4

INGREDIENTS, SALMON STUFFING:

5 ounces of clean salmon flesh
egg white from one egg
1 cup of heavy cream
1 teaspoon of salt
1 pinch of cayenne pepper
a few turns of the white
 pepper-mill
3/4 ounce of chopped truffle
7 ounces of spinach leaves
8 ounces of flaky pastry

INGREDIENTS, SALMON STOCK:

Bones from the salmon
1/2 of a yellow onion
a few sprigs of parsley
1/2 teaspoon of thyme
a few white peppercorns

FOR THE COOKING OF THE SALMON STUFFING:

1 quart of water
a few sprigs of dill
1 teaspoon of salt

FOR BRUSHING:

1 egg yolk

INGREDIENTS, SAUCE:

1/2 cup of heavy cream
1/2 cup of dry white wine
1/2 cup of salmon stock
1 tablespoon of finely chopped
 shallot
3 ounces of butter
salt
a few drops of lemon juice
a few turns of the white
 peppermill
2 large tomatoes
1/2 of a small yellow onion
2 tablespoons of coarsely
 chopped dill

PREPARATION:

Grind the salmon meat in a meat grinder three times through the finest of the steel discs, or in a blender. Place in the refrigerator for a few hours so it cools down completely.

In the meantime, the salmon stock is being prepared: Rinse the salmon bones in running cold water and put them in a saucepan with cold water just covering the bones. Bring to a boil and skim. Put in the sliced onion, the sprigs of parsley, the thyme and the peppercorns and let the liquid simmer for about 20 minutes. Strain.

Bring to a boil one quart of water with a few sprigs of dill and some salt in a wide saucepan and let it cook for a few minutes until the liquid is flavored with the dill. Remove the bowl with ground salmon from the refrigerator. Add one teaspoon of salt. It is very important that the salt be added at once in order to obtain a firm forcemeat. Pour in the egg white and stir vigorously while the cream is added a little at a time. Season with white and cayenne pepper. Mix in the chopped truffle.

With a spoon, shape the forcemeat into four oval balls having roughly the shape of a chicken egg. Place them carefully in the simmering dill liquid and let them simmer for three minutes. Remove them with a slotted spoon and let them cool.

Cook the spinach for a few minutes in lightly salted water. Remove and press out the water. Chop coarsely and sweat in browned butter for a few minutes until most of the liquid has evaporated. Season with salt and pepper and a little ground nutmeg. Place aside to cool.

Out of cardboard cut an oval 5 inches by 3 3/4 inches, and another oval 5 3/4 inches by 4 1/2 inches.

Roll out the flaky pastry dough to 1/10 of an inch. Cut out four ovals from each of the two above described patterns.

On top of each of the smaller ovals, place a bed of spinach. On top of the spinach, place a salmon forcemeat ball. Leave about 1/3 inch border around the oval free and brush with the whipped egg yolk. Place the greater oval on top of the forcemeat and press down along the edges so they stick well together.

The original recipe calls for an "S", 1 3/4 inches by 1/5 inch, and 1/10 inch thick, made of flaky pastry. It is placed on top of the oval package. Brush all of it with the egg yolk. Place on a baking sheet in an oven preheated to 480 degrees F. After 5 minutes, lower the temperature to 400 degrees F. Let it bake for another 10 minutes. With a small sharp knife remove the stem from the tomatoes . Dip them in the boiling dill water and rinse immediately in cold water.

Pull off the skin and divide the tomatoes crosswise. Squeeze the halves so that the seeds are removed. Cut the tomatoes in smaller parts. Sweat the chopped onion in a little butter, but do not let it color. Add the tomato. Season carefully with salt and pepper. Let the mixture cook until all the liquid has evaporated. Work the tomato through a sieve to a paste.

To make the sauce, one cooks the cream, the white wine, the salmon stock and the chopped shallot in a saucepan until about 3/4 cup remains. The onion can be strained out of the sauce (it is not necessary). Take the saucepan away from the stove. Add the butter in small portions while it is being beaten into the sauce. Add the tomato puree. At last mix with 2 tablespoons of coarsely chopped dill. Add a few drops of lemon juice.

Pour the sauce on a plate and place the salmon forcemeat on top.

Werner Vögeli,
Operakällaren,
Stockholm, Sweden

SALMON IN PUFF PASTRY WITH WHITE BUTTER

(Feuilleté de saumon au beurre blanc)

INGREDIENTS:

2 pounds of salmon fillet
1 pound of spinach leaves
4 ounces of mushroom duxelle
2 ounces of chopped shallots
1 cup of dry white wine
1 1/2 pounds of prepared puff pastry
2 bay leaves
1 cup of fish stock
1 dash of nutmeg
2 ounces of butter
1 egg
1 large spoon of white wine vinegar

PREPARATION:

In a large flat pan, combine and boil for 5 minutes:
salmon, white wine, fish stock, bay leaves, chopped shallots, vinegar, salt and pepper. Reserve the stock for the sauce.
Chop the spinach and sauté it in the butter and the nutmeg, then mix in the mushroom duxelle. Knead the puff pastry into a 1/4 inch thick sheet, then cut it into two equal pieces.
Place half of the salmon fillet on one piece of the puff pastry, top it with the mixture of spinach and mushroom duxelle. Place the remaining salmon on top of it. Cover all of it with the second layer of the puff pastry, glueing the edges together with beaten whole egg.
Make a fish scale decoration on top, then glaze it with egg. Bake it in a preheated oven for 30 minutes at 400 degrees F.
Serve with boiled cucumber, string beans (optional) and rice.

Alain P. Sailhac,
Le Cirque,
New York, USA

SALMON BAKED IN PAPER

Serves: 4

INGREDIENTS:

1 pound 4 ounces of fillet of salmon, boned and skinned
1/4 cup of oil, preferably virgin olive oil
salt, white pepper
juice and peel of a fresh lime
fresh ginger
4 sheets of wax-paper

INGREDIENTS FOR VEGETABLE COMPOTE:

1 ounce of butter
1/4 cup of olive oil
3 1/3 ounces of onion (ordinary and shallot)
3 1/3 ounces of carrot
3 1/3 ounces of fresh champignons
3 1/3 ounces of zucchini
1 large tablespoon of coarsely chopped chervil or tarragon
a little fresh ginger
a little white wine

PREPARATION:

Cut the onion, carrot, champignons and zucchini into julienne. First sweat the onion in a mixture of butter and oil for a few minutes, then add the carrot and cook for another 5 minutes, add the champignons and cook for another 2 to 3 minutes. Add the tarragon or the chervil, the ginger, and 1/4 to 1/2 cup of white wine. Cook uncovered until the wine has evaporated. Set aside. Mix the zucchini in the pan. The heat of the dish is enough to warm up the zucchini. Let the compote cool. Divide the fillet of salmon in 4 parts, and then cut each part in 3 equal slices.

Cut out 4 sheets of wax-paper, about 20 x 14 inches each. Fold the paper in two. Place a couple of spoons of the compote on one side of the sheet. Arrange the slices of salmon on top. Sprinkle some salt and some freshly ground white pepper. Place some pieces of the lime peel on top and add some drops of lime juice and some fresh ginger. Brush with oil. Make a tight little package with the paper. Staple at a few places.
Brush a warm baking sheet with a little oil and place the paper packages on the sheet in a preheated oven at 480° F.
Bake for 3 minutes.
Place the packages on the plates and open them at the table.

Eyvind Hellstrøm,
Bagatelle, Oslo, Norway

PAUPIETTE OF SALMON STUFFED WITH CRABMEAT SERVED WITH CEPE BUTTER SAUCE AND FRIED OYSTERS

Serves: 4

INGREDIENTS:

4 escalopes of salmon
 (cut 4 to 5 inches long,
 1/8 inch thick)
salt and pepper

STUFFING INGREDIENTS:

1 branch of celery, sliced
6 medium mushrooms, sliced
1 shallot, sliced
2 tablespoons of butter
2 egg yolks
1 tablespoon of mayonnaise
1 tablespoon of bread crumbs
salt and pepper
8 ounces of lump crabmeat

INGREDIENTS FOR
BUTTER SAUCE:

6 to 8 ounces of cepes, sliced
2 shallots, minced
1 tablespoon of butter
1/4 pound of butter at
 room temperature
salt and pepper
2 ounces of Cognac
1/2 cup of heavy cream
1 tablespoon of parsley, chopped
1 tablespoon of chives, chopped
20 oysters, shucked

METHOD:

To make the stuffing, sauté the celery, mushrooms and shallots. Let cool. Chop fine. Add egg yolks, mayonnaise and bread crumbs. Season to taste with salt and pepper. Fold in crabmeat.

To prepare salmon, lay the strips of fish on table and season with salt and pepper. Divide the stuffing between the four pieces. Roll up the salmon, tucking in the ends. Place in buttered pan and bake at 375 degrees for 10 minutes or until done.
Serve the paupiette on a bed of sauce centered on the plate. Garnish on the outside with 5 fried oysters on each plate.
To make butter sauce: saute cepes and shallots in 1 tablespoon of butter. Salt and pepper. Deglaze with Cognac, add heavy cream and reduce until thick. Blend until smooth in blender. Then return to pan, whisk in the rest of the butter, add parsley and chives.
For fried oysters, use any standard breading (flour, egg wash and bread crumbs). Deep fry or sauté until golden brown.

Steven Mellina,
The Manhattan Ocean Club,
New York, USA

GRAVLAKS IN FLAKY PASTRY

Serves: 4

INGREDIENTS:

1 pound of gravlaks,
 in 12 pieces
24 thin squares of flaky pastry
1/2 pound of spinach, whole
2 cups of white wine sauce
1 2/3 ounces of butter
1 yellow onion
1 egg
salt and pepper

PREPARATION:

Skin the salmon and divide the fish into 12 pieces.
Place each piece of salmon on a pastry square. Chop the onion and saute in butter until soft. Add the coarsely chopped spinach. Season with salt and pepper. Distribute the onion and spinach on the salmon. Place the remaining pastry pieces on top of the salmon fillings. Press the edges well together and brush with the beaten whole egg.
Place on a baking sheet in a pre-heated oven at 300° F for 50 minutes.
Serve with the white wine sauce.

PLANKED SALMON STEAKS

Serves: 4

INGREDIENTS:

4 salmon steaks
2 tablespoons of melted butter
2 tablespoons of lemon juice,
 freshly squeezed
1 teaspoon of salt
1/2 teaspoon of paprika
hot seasoned mashed potatoes
peas with tiny whole onions
dash of pepper
lemon and parsley, if desired

PREPARATION:

Place fish in a single layer on a preheated, oiled wooden plank or a well-greased broil-and-serve platter. Combine butter, lemon juice and seasonings; pour over fish. Bake at 350° F for 25 minutes or until fish flakes easily when tested with a fork. Arrange hot potatoes and vegetables around fish. Garnish with parsley and lemon, if desired.

SALMON ROLLS IN HONEY SAUCE WITH BROCCOLI

Serves: 4

INGREDIENTS FOR THE SALMON:

4 escalopes of salmon,
 4 2/3 ounces each
salt and pepper
butter
16 green peppercorns
16 red peppercorns

INGREDIENTS FOR THE SAUCE:

1 cup of dry white wine
1/4 cup of Noilly Prat
1/2 cup of fish stock
1 1/2 cups of cream
lemon juice
2 ounces of salted butter
2 teaspoons of honey
salt and cayenne pepper

GARNISH:

5 ounces of broccoli flowerets
olive oil
salt

PREPARATION OF THE SAUCE:

Reduce the white wine, the Noilly Prat, the fish stock and the honey. Add cream and cook. Work in the butter. Season with salt, cayenne pepper and lemon juice.

PREPARATION OF THE GARNISH:

Cook the broccoli in salted water with a little olive oil, but keep the broccoli crisp. Remove and set aside.

PREPARATION OF THE SALMON:

Season the fillets with salt and pepper, and roll them into rolls. Pierce them with a tooth pick to keep them together. Butter a fire-proof dish and bake the rolls in a hot oven 2 to 3 minutes on each side.

SERVING:

Place the rolls on plates, warm the broccoli in butter for a short time, season and arrange the broccoli around the salmon. Sprinkle the peppercorns over the salmon and spoon the warm sauce around the fish.

Michael Oberleiter,
La Fontaine,
Wolfsburg, West Germany

STUFFED SALMON IN FLAKY PASTRY WITH SAUCE VERTE

Serves: 4

INGREDIENTS:

1/2 pound of flaky pastry
1/2 egg yolk
5 1/3 ounces of salmon, one half of a skinless fillet (to go inside the pastry)

INGREDIENTS FOR THE SALMON STUFFING:

1 1/3 ounces of salmon fillet
salt, freshly ground pepper
1/3 to 1/2 ounce of cream
2 teaspoons of whipped cream

INGREDIENTS FOR THE TURBOT STUFFING:

2 1/3 ounces of turbot fillet
salt, freshly ground pepper
3/4 to 1 ounce of cream
4 teaspoons of whipped cream
1/5 ounce of diced morels
1/3 ounce of diced carrot, blanched
1/2 tablespoon of finely chopped dill

INGREDIENTS FOR THE SAUCE VERTE:

1 egg yolk
3/4 ounce of oil
1/4 teaspoon of mustard
salt, freshly ground pepper
lemon juice
1/2 teaspoon of dill
1/2 teaspoon of parsley
1/2 teaspoon of tarragon
1/2 teaspoon of sorrel
1/4 teaspoon of chervil

PREPARATION OF THE PASTRY:

The flaky pastry dough should be thoroughly worked in order to have a firm consistency and to prevent it from splitting. Set aside to cool.
The salmon fillet should be precisely cut to fit the pastry. All the trimmings are to be used for the stuffing.

PREPARATION OF THE SALMON STUFFING:

Cut the fillet into thin strips, season with salt and freshly ground white pepper and set aside to chill thoroughly. Process little by little in a thoroughly chilled processor together with ice cold cream until ready. Season and rub it through a fine sieve. Cover and set aside in the refrigerator. Fold in the lightly salted whipped cream with a wooden spoon.

PREPARATION OF THE TURBOT STUFFING:

Cut the turbot fillet into thin strips, season with salt and pepper and set aside to chill thoroughly. Together with the cream, process the mixture to a forcemeat. Season and rub through a fine sieve. Chill thoroughly. Fold in the lightly salted whipped cream and divide the forcemeat in two. Mix one of the portions of forcemeat with the finely diced morels and the blanched diced carrot. Mix the other half of the mixture with the finely chopped dill to give it a tender green color. In order to test the consistency and the taste of the stuffing, drop a small dab of the stuffing into lightly salted boiling water. The poached dab should be tasty and light. If it is not, season again and add some more whipped cream.

PREPARATION OF THE PIE:

Roll the pastry dough into a rectangular sheet 1/8 inch thick and of the same length as the salmon fillet. Make a red-white-green base with part of the three stuffings (salmon, white and green turbot), of the same width as the fillet. Season the fillet with salt and freshly ground white pepper, and place it carefully on the base. Arrange the remaining three stuffings, in the opposite color arrangement, green-white-red, on top of the fillet and close the pastry sheet. Brush the pastry with the stirred egg yolk and place pastry decorations on the pie, or make a grid pattern with a fork. Place the pie in a preheated oven at 430° F for 10 minutes. Turn the oven down to 390° and bake for another 20 minutes, until ready.

PREPARATION OF THE SAUCE VERTE:

Make a mayonnaise with the first four ingredients and blend it with the chopped herbs. If desired, the mayonnaise may be replaced with sour cream or yoghurt.

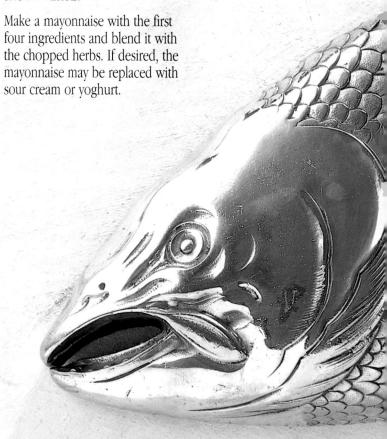

SERVING:

Serve the sliced salmon pie, luke warm, with the sauce on the side.

P.S.:

In order to keep the pastry from running out on the sides, place the pie in a buttered form of strong double aluminum foil which has been folded up on the right and left side of the pie to a height of 2 inches.

*Lothar Buck and
Wolfgang Markloff,
Erbprinz,
Ettlingen, West Germany*

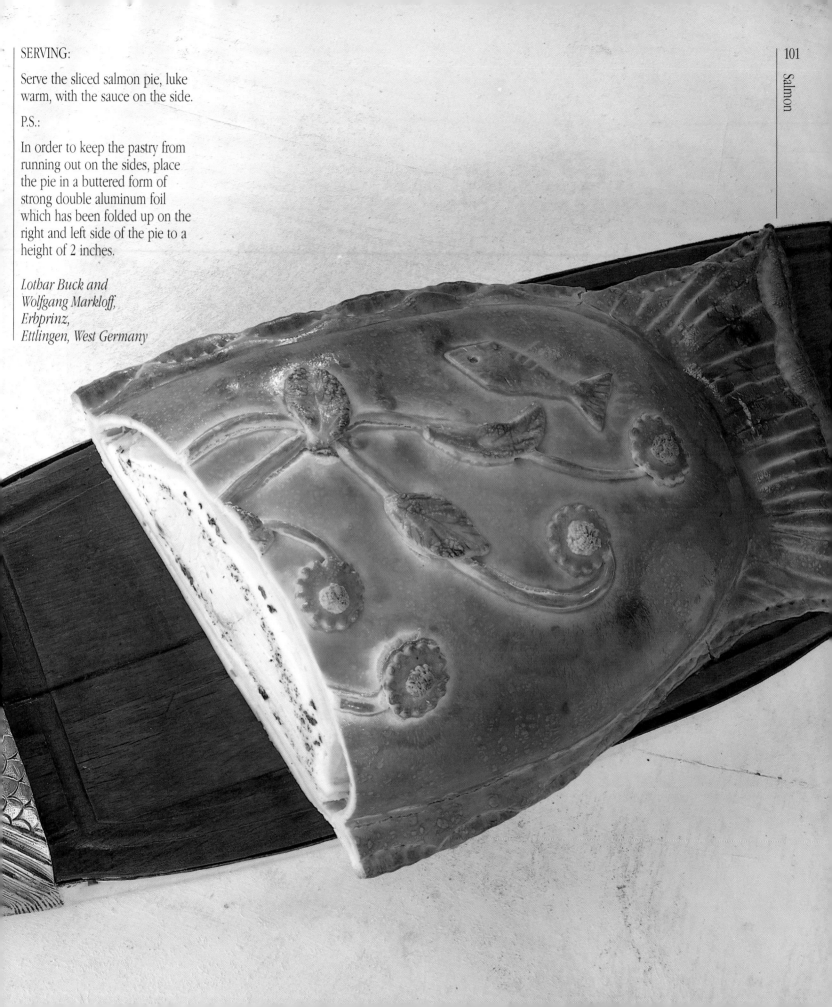

SALMON PIE IN BRIOCHE

Serves: 4

INGREDIENTS:

12 ounces of fillet of salmon,
  skinned and boned, for stuffing
4 ounces of fresh white bread
2 egg whites
7 tablespoons of cream
1 teaspoon of butter
2 ounces of sliced onion
1 teaspoon of salt
white pepper, nutmeg
1 3/4 cups of cream
10 ounces of fillet of salmon,
  used whole
salt, pepper
butter for buttering a bread pan
1 ounce of truffles

INGREDIENTS FOR
THE BRIOCHE:

1 pound of flour
1 ounce of yeast
1/2 cup of milk
5 ounces of butter
2 eggs
1 teaspoon of salt
1/2 teaspoon of sugar

PREPARATION:

Cut away the bread crust. Pour
the egg white and the 7 tablespoons of cream over the bread.
Melt the butter and cook the
onion without giving it color. Put
aside to cool.
Process the first fillet of salmon in
the processor until very fine, but
keep cool all the time. Add the
rest of the cream, a little at a time.
Dice the truffles and add to the
fish.
Line a buttered bread pan with
brioche dough. Fill the pan half
full with the stuffing, place the
whole salmon fillet and cover
with the rest of the ground fish.
On top place a lid made of the
dough, allowing two small
"chimneys". Press the edges well
together. Brush with egg.
Baking time: about 40 minutes.
Oven: 15 minutes in 480° F, the
rest of the time in 430° F.

Walter Nichtawitz,
Lasse's Catering,
Brevik, Norway

SALMON WITH SMOKED SALMON AND HORSERADISH CRUST AND RIESLING CREAM SAUCE

Serves: 4

INGREDIENTS:

4 slices of salmon, 4 ounces each,
  cut from the middle part of a
  large fillet
1 to 2 tablespoons of
  vegetable oil
salt

INGREDIENTS FOR THE CRUST:

2/3 ounce of salted butter
2/3 ounce of sweet butter
1 teaspoon of lemon juice
cayenne pepper
1 tablespoon of shredded
  horseradish
2/3 ounce of smoked salmon,
  best quality, sliced
French bread without crust

INGREDIENTS FOR THE
RIESLING CREAM SAUCE:

1/2 cup of fish stock
1/4 cup of dry Riesling
4 teaspoons of Noilly Prat
  (dry vermouth)
1/2 ounce of heavy cream
1 teaspoon of butter
1 tablespoon of whipped cream
salt, lemon juice and cayenne
  pepper

PREPARATION OF THE CRUST:

Mix the two butters and work
them until they make a nice foam.
Add the lemon juice, cayenne, the
freshly shredded horseradish, the
diced smoked salmon and the
shredded bread. Process in a food
processor.

PREPARATION OF THE SALMON:

Fillet a salmon. Skin one of the
fillets and pull out all the bones
with tweezers. From the middle
part of the fillet cut 4 equal slices
of 4 ounces each. Slightly pound
the thickest part of the slice.
Cover the curved side of the
outside portion of the salmon
slices with crust mixture, 1/5 inch
thick.
Heat some oil in an iron pan.
Place the prepared salmon slices
in the pan, and place this in a
preheated oven under the broiler
until the upper part is brown.
Shut off the broiler and leave the
pan in the oven with the door
slightly open. The salmon should
be pink in the center. To test, the
best way is with a needle. Place
the needle in the fish for 20
seconds. Pull out the needle and
place the part that was in the fish
against the upper lip. The needle
should feel warm, not hot.

PREPARATION OF
THE RIESLING CREAM SAUCE:

Prepare a fish stock with the white
wine and vermouth and reduce.
Add the cream and reduce once
more. Finally, add the butter, the
whipped cream, and season with
salt, lemon juice and cayenne.

SERVING:

Pour sauce on warm plates and
place the salmon in the middle.
Serve at once.
Garnish with whole spinach and a
steamed potato.

Eckart Witzigmann,
Aubergine,
Munich, West Germany

SALMON SOUFFLÉ

Serves: 4

INGREDIENTS:

2 1/2 tablespoons of butter
1 1/2 tablespoons of flour
1/2 tablespoon of Maizena
  (corn starch)
1 pint of boiling milk
1 generous pound of cold cooked
  salmon, boned
4 eggs (2 yolks − 4 whites)
a little chives
a little ground paprika
salt

PREPARATION:

Melt 2 tablespoons of butter in a
small saucepan, stir in the flour
and the Maizena, and mix well
over the fire. Pull the saucepan
aside and pour in the boiling
milk, stir until it is smooth, bring
it to boil and add the finely
chopped salmon, the chives and
the paprika. Mix in the egg yolks
and at last the beaten egg whites
a little at a time with a wooden
spatula.
Butter 4 individual soufflé moulds
with the rest of the butter, pour in
the salmon mixture up to 4/5 of
the mould and bake in the lowest
part of a preheated oven (350
degrees F.) for about 20 minutes.
Serve quickly with white butter or
melted butter.

Willy Wyssenbach,
Continental,
Oslo, Norway

SMALL SALMON BAKED IN FOIL

Serves: 6

INGREDIENTS:

1 small salmon, 3 to 4 pounds
7 ounces of butter
1 cup of fresh parsley greens
1/2 lemon
salt and pepper

PREPARATION OF THE SALMON:

Scrape off the scales on the
salmon with the back of a stiff
knife or a fish scaler, clean and
rinse the fish. Cut off the lower
part of the tail and the fins, but
keep the head on. Dry the fish,
also inside. Season with salt and
pepper inside and out.
Work together 1 2/3 ounces of
butter, softened, a handful of
parsley, the juice of half a lemon,
and distribute it evenly inside the
fish.
Butter a sheet of aluminum foil
with some of the butter, wrap the
salmon in it, and place it in a
baking dish in a preheated oven
(390 degrees F.). After 45
minutes, turn the upper part of
the foil aside to expose the fish,
place a few dabs of butter on top
and move the pan over to the
broiler element in order to make
the fish crisp and golden.
Make a slit in the lower part of
the foil to let out the cooking
liquid, set aside. Place the foil
with the fish on a serving dish
and decorate with parsley at the
head.

PREPARATION OF THE SAUCE:

Pour the stock and the butter
from the baking dish in a small
saucepan, heat well while the
remaining cold butter is beaten
into it. Sprinkle a little parsley
over it.

Willy Wyssenbach,
Continental,
Oslo, Norway

ALMOND BREADED FILLET OF SALMON

Serves: 4

INGREDIENTS:

1 pound 6 ounces of salmon fillets
  from tail part
3 1/2 ounces of flour
3 whole eggs
7 ounces of grated almonds
8 ounces of butter
garden balm according to taste
1 1/2 pounds of steamed
  potatoes

SALAD:
Sundry lettuce greens, with
mustard dressing

PREPARATION:

After the tail part has been
filleted, divide the two fillets
lengthwise in two. Salt the fish,
dip in the flour, the eggs and the
grated almonds.
With a scooping spoon, scoop
out round balls of potatoes or
fashion them with a knife. Prepare
à l'Anglaise.
Rinse the lettuce and prepare a
mixed salad.
Carefully fry the fillets of salmon
until golden brown, about 4 to 5
minutes on each side.
Arrange the fillets on a warm plate
and decorate with the garden
balm.

Walter Nichtawitz,
Lasse's Catering,
Brevik, Norway

CREAM CHEESE-STUFFED SALMON STEAKS

Serves: 6

INGREDIENTS:

6 salmon steaks, one inch thick
4 ounces low-fat cream cheese
2 tablespoons of grated Parmesan
  cheese
1 tablespoon of chopped parsley
1 tablespoon of fresh chopped
  basil, or 1 teaspoon of
  dried basil
1 tablespoon of chopped green
  onion
3 tablespoons of butter, melted
2 tablespoons of lemon juice
salt and pepper to taste
toothpicks

PREPARATION:

Clean, wash and dry the fish. With
a very sharp knife, make an
incision through the skin on the
upper part of the steak where the
fins are located. On each side of
the backbone, make a cut,
forming a pocket to receive the
stuffing. Set aside. Combine
cheeses, parsley, basil and green
onion; blend well. Divide into 6
equal portions. Form each portion
into a flat oval. Place one oval
into the pocket in each steak.
Fasten openings with toothpicks.
Place salmon on well-greased
broiler pan. Combine butter,
lemon juice, salt and pepper.
Baste salmon with butter mixture.
Broil 4 to 5 inches from source of
heat for 4 to 5 minutes; turn.
Baste and cook an additional 4 to
5 minutes, or until salmon flakes
easily when tested with a fork.

MILLE-FEUILLE OF SALMON WITH CHERVIL

(Mille-feuille de saumon au
cerfeuil)

Serves: 4

INGREDIENTS:

14 ounces of flaky pastry
14 ounces of thin escalopes of
  salmon (sliced like smoked
  salmon) about 1/8 inch thick
1 ounce of butter
2 teaspoons of chopped shallots
3/4 cup of dry white wine
1 1/2 cups of cream fleurette
4 tablespoons of chervil leaves
salt and cayenne pepper

PREPARATION OF
THE FLAKY PASTRY:

Roll out the flaky pastry to make a
square, 16 inches by 16 inches,
bake in warm oven.

PREPARATION OF THE SAUCE:

Melt 3/4 ounce butter in a skillet.
Sweat slowly the chopped
shallots. Moisten with white wine
and reduce until dry (complete
evaporation of the liquid). Add
cream fleurette and boil for 4
minutes.

MOUNTING:

Divide the baked pastry sheet
with a bread knife into three
equal strips. Sauté the escalopes
of salmon in a non-stick pan with
very little butter, 2 seconds on
both sides. Place these at regular
intervals on two of the pastry
strips. Place the covered strips on
top of each other and top with
the third strip. The entire
operation must be executed
rapidly.
With the bread knife, divide the
strip assembly into 4 equal parts.
Mask with boiling sauce and
decorate with chervil.

Louis Outhier,
L'Oasis,
La Napoule, France

DOUBLE CUTLET OF SALMON WITH ANCHOVY SAUCE

Serves: 4

(Use the middle part of a medium sized salmon. Remove skin and bones)

INGREDIENTS:

8 cutlets of salmon,
 3 ounces each
2 ounces of butter
1/2 cup of dry white wine
2 cups of heavy cream
1/4 of a clove of garlic
2 peeled and seeded tomatoes
2 fillets of anchovy
1/3 ounce of butter to warm the
 tomatoes
16 leaves of fresh tarragon
 (or some finely chopped chives)
salt and some finely ground white
 pepper

PREPARATION:

Fillet the middle portion of a medium-sized salmon, removing the skin and the bones. Each fillet is cut into equal cutlets of about 3 ounces each, 1 to 1 1/2 inches thick. Rub the salmon with salt and pepper. On a plate, place 2 pieces with the insides facing each other, so the thick part faces the thin part of the other piece. Bind the parts together with a piece of string around the edges. Warm the butter in a frying pan or a sautoire. Brown the cutlets carefully on both sides and place them in a preheated oven at 350° F for 8 to 10 minutes. Baste the fish 3 to 4 times with the butter while it is being fried.

Place the fish on a serving dish and keep warm. Drain the fat. Add the white wine and the heavy cream and reduce together with the garlic to half the volume. Coarsely chop the tomatoes and the anchovy fillets, separately. Warm the tomatoes in the butter in a new sautoire or a small saucepan. Add some salt, pepper and the anchovy. Strain the sauce and pour it over the tomatoes. Remove the string from the fish, serve with the sauce around the cutlets and decorate the sauce with the tarragon leaves.

Willy Wyssenbach,
Continental,
Oslo, Norway

SALMON WITH SEVRUGA CAVIAR, SALMON ROE, WINTER TRUFFLES AND ASPARAGUS SAUCE

Into the sauce, swirl half the caviar, roe and truffles. Serve the medallions on top of the sauce. Top each medallion with caviar, roe and truffles. Place a tomato rose in the center of the plate, with medallions around it.

Andrew Pappas,
The Post House,
New York, USA

Serves: 6

INGREDIENTS:

2 pounds of fresh asparagus
10 tablespoons of sweet butter
1 1/2 cups of heavy cream
1 ounce of Sevruga caviar
1 ounce of salmon roe
1 ounce of black winter truffles,
  finely diced
6 portions of salmon,
  3 medallions per portion;
  2 to 3 ounces per medallion
6 tomatoes (for tomato roses)

METHOD:

Wash and discard ends of asparagus. Cut stalks in half and plunge the top halves into boiling water. Cook until tender. Drain well. Place in blender. Purée with half of the butter until finely puréed. Cut remaining asparagus into small pieces. Simmer them with cream for 20 minutes. Strain through fine sieve. Whisk together asparagus butter and cream. Heat the two together (just below boiling).
Salt and pepper the salmon medallions. In a heavy skillet, heat some sweet butter. When it begins to brown, add the medallions. Brown them on both sides. Reduce heat and cook until desired doneness.

ESCALOPES OF SALMON IN LIME SAUCE WITH GARDEN BALM

Serves: 4

INGREDIENTS:

1 cup of fish stock
1 cup of dry white wine
1 cup of sweet white wine
1/2 star anise
3 ounces of sweet butter
1 ounce garden balm leaves
8 slices of lime
8 escalopes of salmon
 (2 ounces each)
lemon salt
salt and freshly ground pepper

PREPARATION:

Reduce the fish stock and the white wine together with the anise to 1/3. Remove the anise and work into the stock the cold butter, a little at a time. Season with salt and pepper.
Put aside 8 leaves of garden balm for decoration, blanch the rest quickly in boiling water, chill, drain and chop finely. Place the lime slices in the sauce and let them draw a few minutes. Season the salmon with lemon salt and finely ground pepper. Fry quickly in a very warm non-stick pan and place on warm plates. Remove the lime slices, stir the balm leaves into the sauce. Pour the sauce over the fish, place the lime on top and decorate with the balm leaves.

Willy Wyssenbach,
Continental,
Oslo, Norway

ESCALOPES OF SALMON WITH LINGONBERRIES, ASPARAGUS, MUSHROOMS AND CRAYFISH

(Escalopes de saumon aux airelles, petit feuilleté de pointes d'asperges aux pleurotes, chartreuse d'écrevisses)

Serves: 6

INGREDIENTS:

1 salmon, 5 1/2 pounds
1 pound of flaky pastry
4 pounds of asparagus, white or green
2 pounds of pleurotes (mushrooms)
1 pint of olive oil
18 crayfish
2 tablespoons of tomato paste
1/2 pint of Cognac
1 pint of Xeres vinegar
1 bunch of tarragon
2 pounds of fish bones, for the stock
3 quarts of heavy cream
5 ounces of fresh lingonberries, if hard to find, cranberries
4 pounds of carrots
1 celeriac
1 pound of haricots verts, extra fine
2 pounds of butter
1 pound of champignons
10 ounces of shallots
1/3 ounce of saffron
1 pint of Noilly Prat
1 pint of white wine
12 eggs (for sabayon)
2 bunches of chives
salt and pepper

PREPARATION:

Fillet the salmon and remove all the small side bones. Skin and cut into nice escalopes, about 5 ounces each. Lightly pound and set aside in a cool place.
Prepare a one pound sheet of flaky pastry, fold 6 times and cut out 6 small diamond-shaped pieces. Decorate the surface and bake.
Peel and clean the asparagus and cook in salted water. Clean the pleurotes, sauté in oil and drain. Remove the intestines of the crayfish (châtrer). Sweat in olive oil, add mirepoix, tomato paste and flambé with Cognac. Add the vinegar, the tarragon and some fish stock. After two minutes of cooking, remove the crayfish and set aside.
Cook the remaining liquid for 10 minutes, strain, reduce, add the cream. Reduce once more, strain and set aside. Make a sabayon separately, add it to the mixture and carefully blend in the rinsed and dried lingonberries. Keep warm without boiling.
Make small sticks of the carrots and the celeriac and poach in water. Also cook the haricots verts.
Butter dariole moulds, line with the vegetables and mask with a little salmon forcemeat, prepared with the salmon trimmings. Cook in a double boiler in the oven. Dice the champignons and sauté in butter with the chopped shallots, the saffron, and some Noilly. Add the cream and reduce. Mix with the shelled crayfish. This mixture will be used to fill the moulds.

SERVING:

Sauté the escalopes in a skillet. Drain on a clean towel.
Mask the serving dish with lingonberry sauce. Place the escalopes on the sauce.
Alternating the garnish, place the crayfish moulds and the flaky pastry diamonds which have been filled with asparagus points and pleurotes around the escalopes with chive butter.

*Jacques Legrand,
Rouvres, France*

ESCALOPES OF SALMON WITH RHUBARB

Serves: 4

INGREDIENTS:

11 ounces of fresh salmon
2 ounces of rhubarb
2/3 ounce of butter
3/4 cup of heavy cream
1/4 cup of water
salt and pepper

PREPARATION:

Cut the salmon into four equal parts, about 3 ounces each. Wash and slice the rhubarb into 2-inch sticks. Melt the butter in a frying pan. Add the rhubarb, water, salt and pepper, and sauté for about five minutes. Add the cream and allow it to thicken a little. At the same time warm up a non-stick frying pan. When it is good and warm, fry the salmon slices with a little salt and pepper for a few seconds on each side. (They should not be thoroughly cooked). Place on heated plates and decorate with the rhubarb and a little of the sauce.

RECOMMENDED WINES:

Torre di Giano riserva, Montrachet, or a fine exclusive white wine with a well-developed aroma (i.e. Malvasia del Collio, Traminer Aromatico dell'Alto Adige, Hermitage, Graves).

*Gualtiero Marchesi,
Milano, Italy*

ESCALOPE OF SALMON WITH CREAMED SORREL

Serves: 4

INGREDIENTS:

1 3/4 pounds of salmon fillet
2 ounces of butter
3/4 cup of good fish stock
3/4 cup of dry white wine
6 tablespoons of vermouth
 (Noilly Prat)
1 cup of heavy sour cream
salt
juice of 1/2 of a lemon
white pepper
2 tablespoons of sorrel julienne

GARNISH:

steamed potatoes
parsley

PREPARATION:

Slice the salmon in escalopes. Remove all the bones and press down on the escalope with the hand to make it flat.
Reduce the fish stock, the white wine and the vermouth to about half of its volume. Add the sour cream and reduce again until about 1 cup is left. Season with salt, lemon juice and white pepper. Add the sorrel julienne and bring to a boil.
Quickly fry the escalopes in butter for about 30 seconds on each side. Distribute the sorrel on 4 very hot plates and place the escalopes on top.
Serve with steamed potatoes and parsley.

Walter Nichtawitz,
Lasse's Catering,
Brevik, Norway

ESCALOPES OF SALMON WITH SUN-DRIED TOMATO BUTTER AND FROGS' LEGS PROVENÇALE

Serves: 4

INGREDIENTS:

1 side from an 8-pound salmon
 (should yield four 8-ounce
 escalopes).
butter and flour

METHOD:

Flour and sauté in whole butter. Try to get salmon golden brown in color, yet medium rare inside.

TOMATO BUTTER:

1/4 pound of butter
8 pieces of sun-dried tomato
salt, pepper to taste
1 teaspoon chopped parsley
1 teaspoon chopped chives
1 teaspoon basil
1/2 teaspoon lemon juice

Purée butter and tomato in blender. Add salt and pepper. Then, fold in parsley, chives and basil, plus lemon juice. Set aside.

FROGS' LEGS PROVENÇALE

8 pairs of frogs' legs
flour and butter
1 teaspoon of Cognac
1 teaspoon of white wine
1/2 of the sun-dried tomato
 butter

Bone the frogs' legs, reserving the meat. Flour and sauté until golden brown, in butter. Pour off cooking butter. Finish frogs' legs in pan, deglazing with Cognac and white wine. Finish with half of the sun-dried tomato butter.

TO SERVE:

Place one escalope of salmon in center of each plate. Arrange frogs' legs around the outside. Put a spoon of the rest of the butter in the center of the fish.

Steven Mellina,
The Manhattan Ocean Club,
New York, USA

FRIED SALMON IN SOUR CREAM

Serves: 4

INGREDIENTS:

4 slices of whole salmon,
 about 6 ounces each, or
4 pieces of fillet of salmon,
 about 5 ounces each
2 ounces of butter
1/2 tablespoon of flour
2 cups of sour cream
1/4 of a lemon
salt and pepper

PREPARATION:

Season salmon with salt and pepper, fry in lightly browned butter on both sides, while the butter is spooned over the fish. Remove from heat and dress the fish on a warm plate after the bone and the skin have been removed from the whole salmon. Stir the flour into the butter with a whisk, replace the pan on the heat and work in the sour cream and cook slowly while constantly stirring. Add the lemon juice. Season to taste and serve the sour cream sauce piping hot with the fish.

Willy Wyssenbach,
Continental,
Oslo, Norway

PAILLARD OF SALMON WITH CHANTERELLES AND BASIL SAUCE

Serves: 6

INGREDIENTS:

3 pounds of salmon fillet
10 shallots, peeled and minced
2 cups of fresh basil,
  cleaned and chopped
6 medium white mushrooms,
  cleaned and sliced
1 pound of fresh chanterelles,
  cleaned, stems trimmed
1 cup of dry white wine
1 cup of heavy cream
1 quart of fish stock
1/2 pound of sweet butter
3 ounces of vegetable oil
1/4 pound of all purpose flour

METHOD:

In a heavy saucepan, lightly sauté shallots, mushrooms and one cup of basil, for 3 minutes. Deglaze with white wine and reduce to 1/4 cup. Add the fish stock and reduce by half. Add beurre manié, small pieces at a time, until consistency will coat the back of a spoon. (Not all the beurre manié will be necessary, but can be reserved for future use). Add heavy cream and simmer for 20 minutes. Strain through a fine sieve. Add remaining chopped basil. Salt and pepper to taste.

INGREDIENTS FOR FISH STOCK:

1/8 pound of sweet butter
1 onion, peeled and diced
  (medium size)
1 celery stalk, diced
  (medium size)
1 leek, washed thoroughly, diced
  (medium size)
1 pinch of thyme
1 bay leaf
2 tablespoons of crushed black
  pepper
3 pounds of red snapper, striped
  bass or flat fish bones
1 cup of white wine

METHOD FOR FISH STOCK:

Heat butter in a stock pot until it is melted. Add all the vegetables and herbs. Sweat for 5 minutes with cover. Add fish bones and white wine. Cover and sweat for 5 more minutes. Cover with water and bring to a simmer. Simmer for 45 minutes, slowly. Strain stock and return to stove. Reduce until one quart of stock remains.

METHOD FOR BEURRE MANIÉ:

Combine 1/4 pound of butter and 1/4 pound of flour in a mixing bowl. Knead the mixture by hand, until smooth. Refrigerate.

METHOD FOR PAILLARDS OF SALMON:

Salmon should be filleted, then cut on extreme bias into 8-ounce portions. Place the salmon portions between plastic wrap and lightly pound the pieces until about 1/8 inch thick.
In a separate saucepan, sauté the chanterelles in two tablespoons of sweet butter until golden brown on all sides. Add salt and pepper to bring out the natural flavor.

At the last possible moment, heat a large saucepan coated with vegetable oil until it smokes. Quickly place a portion of salmon in the pan. Sauté 30 seconds on each side.
Serve the salmon on top of the sauce. Mount the chanterelles on top of the salmon, and place some fresh basil leaves around the mushrooms.

Andrew Pappas,
The Post House,
New York, USA

SALMON SERVED AS IN BASEL BY THE RHINE

Serves: 4

INGREDIENTS:

4 salmon steaks, 7 ounces each
juice from 1/2 lemon
1 1/3 ounces of flour
2 2/3 ounces of butter
2 cups of white wine
1 cup of meat stock
4 ounces of finely sliced onion
watercress and 4 lemon sections
 for decoration
salt and pepper

PREPARATION:

Sprinkle lemon juice on both
sides of the salmon steaks, season
with salt and pepper, turn over in
flour. Fry the fish in butter until
the bones can easily be removed.
Place the salmon on a serving
dish and keep warm. Drain the
fat. Pour the white wine and the
stock in the pan and reduce to
1/3 of the volume, work in a little
butter and put the sauce aside.
Season the onion with salt, turn it
in flour, place on a grid so the
superfluous flour can be shaken
off. Brown some butter in a frying
pan, add the onion and fry to
golden brown, stirring constantly
with a fork.
Distribute evenly the fried onion
on the salmon steaks.
Decorate the dish with watercress
and the lemon sections.
Strain the sauce and serve on the
side.

Willy Wyssenbach,
Continental,
Oslo, Norway

Salmon

SALMON ON FLAKY PASTRY

(Mille-feuille de saumon)

Serves: 4

Time for preparation: 30 minutes
Time for cooking: 40 minutes

INGREDIENTS:

one sheet of flaky pastry
  (8 inches by 12 inches)
8 escalopes of salmon, about
  2 ounces each, wide and thin
1 1/2 cups of fish stock with
  champagne
1 cup of whipped butter
a few sprigs of chervil
1/2 cup of olive oil
salt and pepper
1 pound of sugar peas in their
  pods (if possible)
2 2/3 ounces of butter

PREPARATION AND COOKING:

Bring the peas to a boil in salted
water. Rinse in cold water, drain
and blanch in the 2 2/3 ounces of
butter. Bake the flaky pastry sheet
and cut it into 12 rectangles.
Reduce the fish stock with champagne, beat in the whipped butter
and let the chervil infuse in the
liquid.
Heat some olive oil in a pan until
it smokes. Sauté the salmon
escalopes on high heat.

ON THE PLATE:

Make a bed of sugar peas on the
first flaky pastry rectangle, and
place an escalope of salmon on
top. Mask with chervil butter.
On top, place another rectangle
of flaky pastry, with an escalope
of salmon on it, masking it with
the chervil butter. Place a pastry
rectangle on top and mask it with
the butter.

Alain Chapel,
Mionnay, France

SALMON WITH TRUFFLES AND LEEKS

(Le saumon aux truffes et aux poireaux)

Serves: 4

INGREDIENTS:

1 fillet of salmon, one pound
4 leeks
2 2/3 ounces of butter
2/3 ounce of truffles
1 cup of truffle stock
salt, pepper and lemon
1/2 cup of olive oil

PREPARATION OF THE SALMON AND THE LEEKS:

Salmon:
Cut the salmon in 4 equal slices. Brush it with olive oil and season with salt and pepper. Set aside.
Leeks:
Remove the root and the dark green tops. Slice it into fine slices. Wash it well to remove all the soil. Drain well.

PREPARATION OF THE TRUFFLE BUTTER:

Process the truffles and 3/4 of the butter in a blender.

COOKING OF THE SALMON AND THE LEEKS:

Place the slices of the salmon in a lukewarm non-stick pan and fry slowly on one side. The salmon should be pink after cooking. In the meantime, cook the leeks in a saute pan with the remaining butter and a little water. Let it cook for 5 minutes. Heat the truffle stock and beat it into the truffle butter. Season with salt, pepper and a few drops of lemon.

SERVING:

Drain the leeks and the fish slices and sponge with a paper towel. Place the leeks in the middle of a dish and the salmon on top. Mask with the sauce.

Bernard Loiseau,
La Côte-d'Or,
Saulieu, France

SALMON GRATIN WITH MUSTARD AND GREEN PEPPER

Serves: 4

INGREDIENTS:

4 whole slices of salmon with skin and bones, about 6 ounces each
3 1/2 ounces of butter
1 1/3 ounces of canned green pepper, coarsely chopped
4 tablespoons of French mustard
1 egg yolk
dry grated bread
1/2 cup of light brown meat stock
1 1/3 ounces of leek julienne (white part) 1 inch long
1 1/3 ounces of carrot julienne
salt and pepper

PREPARATION:

If necessary, dry the fish with kitchen or paper towels, season with salt and pepper while the butter is being lightly browned in the pan. Lightly brown the salmon on one side. Turn over and place the pan in a preheated oven to 350° F. Baste with the butter several times until the fish is ready and the backbone can be removed.
Place the fish on a fire-proof dish or plate, remove the bones, the skin, and press a mixture of green pepper, mustard and egg yolk on the salmon. Sprinkle the grated bread, place under the broiling element in a hot oven for about 1/2 minute.
Serve with the meat stock around the fish and place the butter-blanched vegetables in the opening of the fish.

Willy Wyssenbach,
Continental,
Oslo, Norway

SALMON WITH WATERCRESS AND CHIVE BUTTER

(Le Saumon à la tombée de cresson et au beurre de ciboulette)

Serves: 4

INGREDIENTS:

1 fillet of salmon, one pound
2 bunches of watercress
2 small bunches of chives
4 ounces of butter
1/2 cup of olive oil
salt, pepper and lemon

PREPARATION OF THE WATERCRESS:

Undo the bunches and separate the leaves from the stems.

PREPARATION OF THE CHIVE BUTTER:

With a knife, cut the chives into thin slices. Put 3 1/3 ounces of butter in the blender and add the chives. Blend. Set aside in a cool place.

PREPARATION OF THE SALMON:

Cut the salmon in four equal parts. Season. Brush with olive oil.

Salmon

COOKING THE SALMON AND THE WATERCRESS:

Place the salmon pieces in a luke-warm non-stick pan and fry them very slowly on one side.
In the meantime, boil the watercress in a little water with a good tablespoon of butter. Season with salt and pepper.
While the salmon and the watercress are being cooked, prepare the chive butter. Heat 3/4 cup of water in a small pan. When the water boils, beat in the chive butter with a whisk. Season with salt, pepper, and a few drops of lemon juice.
When the salmon is cooked (it should be pink), dry it with a paper towel. Do the same with the watercress. Place the watercress on a dish, put the salmon on it, and the chive butter around the salmon.

Bernard Loiseau,
La Côte-d'Or,
Saulieu, France

SALMON WITH ALMONDS AND CURRY SAUCE

Serves: 4

INGREDIENTS:

1 pound 5 ounces of salmon fillet
1/4 cup of milk
1 ounce of flour
1 1/2 ounces of finely chopped or grated almonds
2 1/2 ounces of butter
1 1/2 ounces of almonds, sliced
1 cup of curry sauce
salt

PREPARATION:

Cut the salmon in four or eight pieces, salt and turn them in the milk. Mix the flour and the grated almonds. Turn the fish in this mixture, pressing with the hand so that the mixture sticks to the fish.
Fry the salmon on both sides in lightly browned butter. Place on a dish or a plate and keep warm. Clean the pan, brown the remaining butter and fry the sliced almonds to a golden brown, constantly stirring with a table fork. Drain all the fat and arrange the almonds on top of the salmon.
Serve with the curry sauce.

Willy Wyssenbach,
Continental,
Oslo, Norway

SALMON STEAK WITH DILL CHARDONNAY BUTTER

Serves: 6

INGREDIENTS:

10 shallots, peeled and minced
1/2 pound of sweet butter
10 medium white mushrooms, cleaned and sliced
1/2 bunch of fresh dill (discard large stems and clean). Reserve 1/2 cup for garnish
2 tablespoons of white vinegar
2 cups of dry white Chardonnay wine
1 cup of heavy cream
salt and white pepper
6 salmon steaks, 3/4 inch thick

METHOD:

In a heavy saucepan, lightly sauté the shallots in one tablespoon of butter until aroma is noticed. Add mushrooms and dill. Sauté one minute. Deglaze with white vinegar and reduce until dry. Add wine and reduce to 2 table-spoons. Add cream and boil until slightly thickened (about 5 minutes). Remove from heat and whisk in remaining butter (small pieces, one at a time).
Strain sauce through fine sieve. Chop remaining dill and add it to the sauce for garnish and taste. Season with salt and white pepper.
Salt and pepper the salmon steaks. Melt one tablespoon of sweet butter in a heavy skillet. When the butter begins to brown, add the salmon and brown for about 1 minute. Turn the salmon and fry for 1 more minute.
Place in preheated oven (350° F) for approximately 2 to 3 minutes, depending on its thickness.
Serve salmon steaks on top of the sauce. Garnish with dill sprigs.

Andrew Pappas,
The Post House,
New York, USA

121

SALMON FROM BROILER WITH AVOCADO SAUCE

Serves: 4

INGREDIENTS:

4 slices of salmon
  (about 6 ounces each)
  cut from whole fish
olive oil
2 ripe avocadoes
4 lemon sections
1/2 tablespoon of lemon juice
1 tablespoon of sour cream
1/2 bunch of watercress
salt and pepper

PREPARATION:

Process the avocado meat, the leaves of 1/4 bunch of the watercress, the sour cream and the lemon juice until you have a mousse. Season with salt and pepper. This sauce tastes best when cold, but should not be prepared too long in advance. Season the salmon, brush with olive oil and broil in high heat until the back bone can easily be removed.
Dress the salmon with watercress leaves and lemon sections. Serve the sauce on the side.

Willy Wyssenbach,
Continental,
Oslo, Norway

SALMON FONDUE

Serves: 4

INGREDIENTS:

1 1/3 pounds of boned lean
  salmon, diced in 1-inch cubes
1 pint of oil or 1 pound of
  coconut butter
2 cups of mayonnaise,
  tartare or bearnaise sauce
8 lemon sections
salt and pepper
bread
4 servings of mixed salad

PREPARATION:

Skewer the salmon cubes on fondue forks and fry them in the fat so that they keep a raw core in the middle. Season, sprinkle a little lemon juice, and dip them in one or several of the sauces according to taste. Serve with bread and a salad.

Willy Wyssenbach,
Continental,
Oslo, Norway

SALMON EN BROCHETTE WITH LARGE MUSSELS

Serves: 4

INGREDIENTS:

1 pound 5 ounces of salmon,
  tail part
8 large mussels, shelled

INGREDIENTS FOR SAUCE:

1 onion, finely chopped
1/4 cup of Pernod
1 cup of cream
8 ounces of butter
1/4 cup of white wine
salt, mustard seeds,
  finely chopped dill

GARNISH:

Wild rice and salad

PREPARATION:

Use the tail part of a salmon, from the vent. Season with salt and pepper and refrigerate for 24 hours. Dice the fish in one inch cubes. Place the salmon cubes and the mussels on a skewer. Sweat the chopped onion in butter, add the white wine. Reduce, add the cream and the mustard seeds. Reduce the mixture to a creamy consistency and season with salt and dill. Cook the wild rice as indicated on the package.
Broil the salmon and mussels on a charcoal grill. Place on a warm pan or dish and flambé with Pernod.
Arrange the wild rice on a warm plate or dish. Place the skewer on top. Pour sauce in flambé pan and add Pernod. Add butter gradually.
Arrange the sauce carefully around the rice.
Serve with a salad.

Walter Nichtawitz,
Lasse's Catering,
Brevik, Norway

GRAVLAKS FROM THE GRILL

Serves: 4

INGREDIENTS:

1 pound of gravlaks with the skin
4 teaspoons of oil
1 cup of mustard sauce
 (see page 33)

Cut the salmon in 8 thick slices,
reserve the skin which is cut in
strips. Brush the slices with oil
and turn them quickly on a warm
grill. The skin that ahead of time
has been scraped clean of the
scales, is grilled and served
together with the salmon.

Willy Wyssenbach,
Continental,
Oslo, Norway

INGREDIENTS

AMERICAN	BRITISH
anise	aniseed
asparagus points	asparagus spears
balm	lemon balm
basilicum	basil
beet	beetroot
Belgian endive	chicory
bell pepper	green or red pepper
Boston sole	replace with Dover sole
celery root	celeriac
champignons	button mushrooms
chicory	curly endive
cornstarch/starch	cornflour
cream – heavy	double cream
– light	single cream
– sour (may be substituted for crème fraîche, but may separate if used in sauces)	soured cream (may be substituted for crème fraîche, but may separate if used in sauces)
flaky pastry (Phyllo dough can be successfully substituted)	puff pastry
ground red pepper	cayenne pepper
lemon salt	dried salt flavoured with finely grated lemon zest
lingonberries	replace with cranberries
lumpfish fillet	replace with white fish fillet
onions – green	spring onion
– white	ordinary onion
– yellow	Spanish onion
parsley greens	parsley
powered sugar	caster sugar
purslane	replace with sorrel or spinach
red beet	beetroot
scallion	spring onions
semolina	ground rice
shrimps	prawns
snow peas	mangetout
squash	replace with courgettes
sugar peas	young mangetout
sweet butter	unsalted butter
thistle oil	replace with sunflower oil
whipped butter	replace with softened butter
wheat flour	wholemeal flour
white radish	Daikon (Japanese radish)
Xeres vinegar	replace with white wine vinegar
zucchini	courgettes

MISCELLANEOUS

baking pan	roasting tin
bread pan	loaf tin
broil	grill
cake pan	sandwich tin
fire	flame
plastic foil/wrap	cling film
skillet	frying pan
wax paper	non-stick paper

SALMON

INTERNATIONAL
CHEFS' RECIPES